"Jeanene Reese has written a truthfu[...] opportunities and the challenges men and women confront as they seek to establish authentic partnerships in every sector of their lives. Ms. Reese provides a refreshing and positive perspective as she suggests ways that men and women might effectively collaborate in order to contribute to the greater common good. *Bound & Determined* serves as an important reminder of the need to diligently seek understanding and cooperation among all people."

—**Kim S. Phipps**, president of Messiah College

"As an author who has been urging Christians for forty years to bring their gender relations practices and beliefs under the scrutiny of Scripture, it pleases me greatly to see younger biblical scholars rise to the challenge and make their contribution to the discussion. Many books are being published that advocate a destructive view of gender roles, destructive because based on the evil consequences of the fall.

Dr. Reese clearly rejects such aberrations and builds her biblical case on God's original designs in creation and on their confirmation with the advent of the new creation in Christ. She draws from the purity of both models the proposal of partnership relations of mutuality as the biblical norm for gender relations. Her work is based on a respectful and holistic view of Scripture, on life experiences freshly presented, on the results of classroom participation, and on insights gained from interaction in the family circle. The result is a lively and persuasive introduction to the vision of God's community lived out in church and family as a partnership of grace rather than in the brokenness of hierarchy."

—**Gilbert Bilezikian**, professor of biblical studies emeritus, Wheaton College

"In *Bound & Determined*, Jeanene Reese shifts our paradigm from that of the individual leader to that of leading together across the gender divide. Based on scriptural insights, research from her classroom, and her own years of partnering with men in ministry, Dr. Reese provides biblical and practical lessons that will enhance the partnerships of women and men in ministry, in schools, and in the family. As a pastoral leader of a mega church with responsibilities for developing leaders and ministry infrastructure, I will find these principles for growing partnerships particularly helpful for me and my team as we continue to strengthen our collaborative leadership practices. *Bound & Determined* will prove to be a valuable resource for every man and woman committed to working and serving together!"

—**Dr. Jeanne Porter**, author of *Leading Ladies and Leading Lessons*,
assistant pastor of Apostolic Church of God, Chicago, IL

Bound & Determined

Bound & Determined

CHRISTIAN MEN AND WOMEN IN PARTNERSHIP

Jeanene Reese

LEAFWOOD
PUBLISHERS

BOUND & DETERMINED
Christian Men and Women in Partnership

LEAFWOOD
P U B L I S H E R S

Copyright 2010 by Jeanene Reese

First edition

978-0-89112-678-2

Printed in the United States of America

LIBRARY OF CONGRESS CATALOGING-IN-PUBLICATION DATA
Reese, Jeanene.
 Bound and determined : Christian men and women in partnership / Jeanene Reese.
-- 1st ed.
    p. cm.
ISBN 978-0-89112-678-2
 1. Sexism--Religious aspects--Christianity. 2. Sex role--Religious aspects--Christianity.
3. Man-woman relationships--Religious aspects--Christianity. 4. Interpersonal relations--
Religious aspects--Christianity. I. Title.
BT708.R425 2010
277.3'083082--dc22

                                                          2010017062

Cover design by Rick Gibson
Interior text design by Sandy Armstrong

Leafwood Publishers is an imprint of
Abilene Christian University Press
1626 Campus Court
Abilene, Texas 79601
1-877-816-4455
www.leafwoodpublishers.com

09 10 11 12 13 14 / 7 6 5 4 3 2 1

Bound & Determined
is dedicated to
Jack,
my husband and life partner,
in love,
in life,
in ministry.

Table of Contents

Acknowledgments

So many different people have partnered with me in this project that I hesitate to mention any of them for fear of leaving someone significant out. Let me begin by thanking my family, who not only served me faithfully as I completed my doctoral studies but have borne patiently with me as I continued the research represented in this book.

Jack, my husband, to whom the book is dedicated, is responsible for the title and is referenced numerous times in my writing. I couldn't have done it without him. I want to thank our oldest daughter, Jessica, and her husband, Jonathan, for giving me two precious granddaughters during the course of this writing project. Also, Jessica served as my primary editor, and I credit her with making the material publishable.

Many thanks belong to Jocelyn, our middle daughter, and her husband, Mark. My work was conducted during most of Jocelyn's high school and college years, and she has been a real trooper through it all. Mark was a student in the team-taught classes discussed in the book and therefore a contributor to the project. I also appreciate Jay, our son, who has taught me so much about what it takes for a boy to grow into a man. I love all of you and thank you for your love and support of me and of this work.

I also want to express gratitude to David Wray, Robert Oglesby, and Sonny Guild, who worked with me in the team-taught courses. Thanks goes to my administrative assistants and graduate assistants: Ryan Maloney, David Kneip, Nathan Zinck, Kaylynn Nossaman Myers, Naomi Cochran Walters, and Amanda Taylor Pittman, and numerous other students from ACU's Graduate School of Theology who served as focus group facilitators and recorders. I couldn't have conducted the research without all of you. I am equally appreciative of all the students who worked with us as we conducted our research. I hope that you have learned as much through it as I have and that you are still learning about godly partnership between women and men.

I would like to thank Jerry Taylor for writing the foreword and for being such an encouraging partner to me in our work together. I am grateful to work in the College of Biblical Studies, where daily I am blessed to partner with some amazing and godly people.

Finally, I wish to express appreciation to Leonard Allen and Heidi Nobles, who made publication possible, and to the individuals who endorsed the book.

Jeanene Showed Up and God Showed Out

Dr. Jerry Taylor

The 2006 New Wineskins Retreat in Malibu, California, was an unforgettable experience. The retreat is an annual gathering of primarily African American ministers and church leaders. It seeks to provide a healthy environment conducive for growth, refreshment, and healing among leaders who are discouraged by an often restrictive religious system.

As we planned the Malibu retreat, it dawned on me that in all of my years of hearing the debate over the role of women in the church, I had never seen women invited to actively participate in the discussion, not to mention lead it. Typically men discussed women's leadership roles while the women sat passively and quietly. In every sense, we failed to partner with our sisters in Christ in this important discussion. As I confronted this realization, I began to see clearly that Christian partnership between men and women was a moral issue.

How could we men have a discussion about women without providing a platform for them to speak in their own voices concerning issues that impact them the most? It would be unthinkable in America today, or at least it should be, to have a discussion about the involvement of African

Americans in the life of the church without providing a space for African Americans to speak in their own voices. So it should be for women.

Working from this insight, I suggested to the planning committee that we conduct the discussion a bit differently than we had approached it in the past. Instead of asking only males to lead the discussion, we would ask all women to be the main presenters and tell us what they thought we most needed to hear. The planning committee readily accepted the idea.

When we started thinking of women who could bring profound insights and brilliant scholarship to the subject, Jeanene Reese's name was among the first we considered. I knew we were on the right track in seeking her participation. I have been fortunate over the years to observe how she consistently displays outstanding leadership and collegiality with grace and strength as a female faculty member in an overwhelmingly male department. The other male faculty and I have benefited personally, spiritually, and professionally as a result of Jeanene's effective mentoring and encouragement.

On that historic day in Malibu, Jeanene stood with three other powerful women of God to courageously address a mostly male audience. As Jeanene spoke in a strong but non-accusatory fashion, it seemed to me that the men discerned her genuine spirit of partnership and solidarity with them. It was special to witness Jeanene's powerful presentation impacting African American men in such a profound way. I think one of the reasons this audience was able to connect with Jeanene as a woman is that African American men are quite familiar with the painful effects of their own marginalization in a majority white society.

Jeanene delivered a memorable message on that occasion, one that had a lasting influence on all those present. As she spoke, it became evident to me that something extraordinary was unfolding in the dynamic exchange between Jeanene and the audience. There seemed to be an electrical current running throughout her presentation that ignited what is known in the Black Church tradition as the "call and response."

I had observed this rhythmic give-and-take between the speaker and the audience in the Black Church all of my life. This, however, was the first time I witnessed a call and response taking place between a white female speaker and a predominately black male audience.

I asked myself the question, how could such a powerful moment like this happen? It dawned on me that Jeanene's God-given approach made it possible. She came across as a colleague and not as a competitor. She spoke as an equal and not as an inferior. I noticed the complete absence of fear, judgment, and condemnation in her voice as she expressed her point of view. It was clear that she felt she was in a safe place, among friends who desperately wanted and needed to hear what she had to say on an extremely important subject. It was as if Jeanene's soul transcended her personality as it became increasingly clear that God was doing something uniquely special with her.

In that sacred moment, she became owned by the Word and, therefore, she became "our" speaker. As she spoke with passion, her words inspired life into the broken places within us as men, primarily, and also as African Americans. The spoken Word made it impossible for us to refrain from loudly shouting "yes" to the truth she so effectively proclaimed. We collectively sensed that God was using Jeanene as a mouthpiece for righteousness and truth at such a historic moment.

This holy happening, this sacred occurrence, this major moment in time mediated through a woman of God motivated men of God to stand on their feet in enthusiastic celebration with their voices raised in unfettered joy. I believe that it was at this moment that it became crystal clear to the mainly male audience that the Word of Life still finds free course through all God's children, regardless of gender.

Joseph and Zachariah, the earthly fathers of Jesus and John the Baptist, were blessed to witness the giving of new life through a woman as God's instrument, and in the interchange at this retreat and ever afterward, so were we.

Introduction

Our whole family was home for a visit. We were seated around the dining room table after enjoying a wonderful meal and great conversation. We lingered awhile, no one wanting to spoil the pleasant experience or do the dishes. While we sat there, I looked across the table at our great-niece Brynn and was taken back several years—she looked a whole lot like our oldest daughter Jessica at the same age.

I mentioned the resemblance, and soon we all moved to the living room, still ignoring the dirty kitchen, and began to look through family photo albums. Sure enough, Brynn and Jessica looked amazingly alike. They still do. We discovered that our oldest granddaughter Simone favors her Aunt Joci (our middle daughter Jocelyn). We enjoyed looking at Jay, the youngest of our children, in the many costumes he loved to play in as a little boy. (He's an actor now.) We laughed at early pictures of Jack and me in college and relived the weddings of Jonathan and Jessica and Mark and Jocelyn. As we looked at each photograph, we began to tell the stories behind them—where we had lived, what the occasions had been, who the other people were in the pictures, and what made our being together so memorable.

Eventually, the children needed to go to bed, the dishes had to be washed, and we all needed to get some sleep. We said our good nights and ended a lovely evening that would linger in our memories for quite some time.

It has been ten months since I sent *Bound & Determined* to the publisher. I purposefully did not look at any of it during that time because I had several other projects that needed my attention and because I needed some distance from the book. I am better able to give and receive edits if I am not too attached to the material being edited.

As I have now revisited each chapter and developed the study guide, I have much the same feeling that I did that night in our living room as we looked at family photo albums. Many of the stories or examples in the book take place over a forty-year span. (Now, that makes me feel really old!) When re-reading them, I picture the people, places, and situations they represent. In reviewing the biblical material presented throughout the book, I am reminded of the first time I studied those passages or where I taught them. Preparation of the study guide caused me to stop and pray about my partnerships and areas in which I still need to learn and grow. I recognize again that as Christian women and men we are bound together by God's design and that we live with a determination to be God's holy people in all of our partnerships.

I would like to invite readers to look through this photo album with me, see the pictures of partnerships that I see and add their own unique ones. In Chapter One, I share a sacred moment in partnership that in many ways caused me to undertake this project. It caused me to go back to Genesis and look at God's design for men and women from the beginning. The result is a theology of partnership that informs everything else in the book.

In this book's foreword, Jerry Taylor refers to the story that also opens Chapter Two. It is about an electrifying experience we shared at a preacher's retreat where three other women and I spoke. What took place there led me to call both women and men to repent of the ways we frequently sin against each other so that we can reclaim what God intends for us.

Chapter Three begins with a social event that set a pattern for how my husband Jack and I often interact in mixed-gender gatherings just to keep things interesting. What follows is the results of an eight-year study I conducted among students I teach at Abilene Christian University about how partnership is developed between and men and women. All of the students were majors in the Department of Bible, Missions, and Ministry and are now spread out across the U.S. and around the world. A description of the study appears in the appendix at the end of the book. I have included various student reflections about their work in partnership in sidebars throughout the book. In many ways, readers are invited to have conversations with those students as much as with me.

The story that begins Chapter Four reflects an experience Jack and I had while ministering to singles at a large church in Memphis. The welcoming and loving nature of that community deeply affected both of us, but it especially changed me. Our time there was short, but the effects of it linger on. The chapter challenges Christians to consider how we engage culture and how our choices affect our views of gender. The discussion concludes with an overview of the kinds of churches that lead the way in fostering godly partnership between women and men.

In Chapter Five, I share a very tender story about my marriages to Jack and my previous husband, Mike Warren, who died in an accident in 1974. What follows is an examination of secular views of marriage, pseudo-Christian views of it, and what I believe is a biblical understanding of marriage that has transformed our lives.

Finally, to begin Chapter Six, I share a teaching experience that turned my world upside down and forced me to seek reconciliation as my way of life. The focus in these pages is on why forgiveness is important when our partnerships fail. In the conclusion, I confess that writing this book has been a special challenge for me. The topic of partnership between women and men was not one that I felt naturally drawn to, yet I felt compelled by God to research it, share my experiences with it, and write about it.

As you look through this album, I hope you see yourself from time to time and envision not just how things are in your life but how, by the power of Christ, they might be. I hope that you will be challenged to think in new ways about how women and men can work together, I pray that God will instruct your heart to form healthier and godlier partnerships. I pray that you will see in this album a vivid picture of God who has been at work, sometimes in hidden ways, not just in my stories but also in yours, and that you might see more clearly the family resemblance—how each of us is being changed more and more into the likeness of God. And mostly I pray that you will recognize we are bound together as Christian women and men by God's design and that we must live with a determination to be God's holy people in all of our partnerships.

Chapter One

A Biblical Theology of Partnership

What God Designed for Us

The energy in the classroom was electric as my two male colleagues and I finished team-teaching our class. We had each shared different ministry experiences from our past and poured our hearts out about the joys and challenges of ministry. We stayed for a few minutes after our class to visit with students but cut it short in order to get home to our families. As we straightened up the room, gathered our materials, and prepared to leave, I was suddenly overwhelmed with emotion. Tears ran down my face while I struggled to gain some sense of control and not appear a stereotypical, overly emotional woman. The response of my two colleagues to my crying, however, speaks volumes about their character and the relationship we share.

They came to my side asking what was wrong, if they had done anything to hurt or offend me. I was so overcome with emotion I could hardly speak. When I finally gained some composure, I tried to explain, "I'm crying because what we have just experienced is how it's supposed to be. We're supposed to be able to work together like this, men and women in this kind of harmony, mutual respect, and partnership." We just stood there for a moment and prayed. We prayed for women and men and the partnerships they form. We prayed about the barriers that divide us, and asked forgiveness for the ways we inevitably hurt each other as men and women. We prayed for our students and their relationships.

For me, that was a sacred moment, one that still deeply affects me and continues to shape the relationship I have with these men and others like them. It also was the beginning of this quest.

———————◦—✦—◦———————

Women and men work together every day in the church—as husbands and wives, brothers and sisters, friends and colleagues. We try to understand and support one another, but we are often left confused, frustrated, or feeling like failures in our interpersonal relationships. Too often, we joke around about our differences or explain them away. Sometimes we give up in despair, or, perhaps worse, we resort to keeping the sexes apart and avoid real and meaningful interaction. It is much simpler to accept that women are from Venus and men from Mars than it is to work through the complexities of our interpersonal relationships. It is easier to accept long-held traditional views than it is to give attention to what Scripture has to say about how and why we come together in these important relations. Yet partnership between men and women is central to God's design for us. I will examine partnership from three central perspectives: a theology of partnership from the creation account in Genesis, a review of the biblical narrative in the Hebrew Bible, and the establishment of a new order in the New Testament.[1]

The Creation Account in Genesis

The most natural starting point for developing a theology of partnership is an examination of God's intention for men and women from the beginning. The creation accounts in Genesis 1 and 2 indicate that God made all humankind, male and female, to bear the creator's image. Mysterious and profound, human beings were formed so that something of the plurality and complexity of God's nature was (and still is) reflected in both. Being female is as much about Godlikeness as being male. Yet many of us did not grow up with this understanding. Reading the creation accounts or telling it to children often means attention given to the activity of each day, to the actual length of a day, or to where the dinosaurs fit in. All important things, and worthy of consideration. Still, our focus tends to be more on what God did than on who God is. No wonder, then, that we miss a sense of bearing God's image. Yet the first two chapters of Genesis are windows that allow us to see who God is and who we are in relationship to God from two distinct perspectives.

Genesis 1 describes an unfolding and powerful scene of God creating and ordering the world. God spoke and something came to be where previously nothing had been. One of my favorite teaching experiences in a children's Vacation Bible School was designing a time travel machine to tell the story of creation. With limited technology (it was the '80s) and a great deal of imagination, we "traveled" back in time to before the earth was formed. Each time we made the journey, the children, who ranged in age from kindergarteners to fifth graders, sat absolutely still in anticipation. Flashing lights, sound effects, and well-placed props helped them experience the creation of light, of vegetation, of animals.

Not once, however, do I think those same children experienced one of God's greatest works: the formation of humanity—male and female—in God's image. As chapter one concludes, God blesses the newly formed human beings and gives them work to do. They were jointly to be fruitful and multiply, to fill the earth and subdue it, and to have dominion together over all things—cultural mandates that give them a great deal of "latitude for creativity and variety."[2]

The narrative of the second chapter alters the order of creation significantly. As a child, I loved to play in the mud, especially at my grandmother's house. An avid gardener, she was always preparing the ground, planting seeds, or harvesting produce. She often put my love for the soil to good use. At other times, I simply made buckets full of "dough" and enumerable "mud pies." These images are always in my mind as I read how God gathered dust, formed the first man, and breathed life into his body. God then placed the man in the garden with orders to tend to it. Recognizing the man's need for partnership, God created the rest of the world and brought all living creatures to be named by the man. Yet none of the animals were suitable partners for the man, so God anesthetized him and performed the first surgery—removing a rib from his side and forming a woman. Some would argue that because the male was created first, God intended for the man to be the leader and the woman the follower. But nothing in the text supports this presupposition. In fact, pastors at wedding ceremonies across denominations routinely use this biblical passage to speak of God's wisdom in making the woman from the man's side instead of his head or his heel, as a sign of her partnership with him. Still others suggest hierarchy in the male/female relationship because the man named the woman as he did the animals, but they miss an important element of the story. According to Marrs:

> When Adam names the animals, the grammatical construction reflects the traditional defining, ordering, and controlling. When Adam names the woman, the grammatical construction changes and the element of exclamation appears. Interestingly, as he excitedly "names" this creature "woman" (*ishshah*), he simultaneously names himself "man" (*ish*).[3]

From the moment he sees her, the man is aware that he has been given a special gift and is appropriately responsive. In naming her and then himself, he immediately recognizes their similarity, their compatibility. Instead of teaching the subordination of woman to man, Genesis 2 demonstrates God's intention for the beauty and uniqueness of mutual interpersonal relationships.

In the creation narrative, the woman is designed to be a helper/ partner to the man. Interestingly, it is the man that God commands to leave father and mother and cleave to his wife (2:24). This directive countermands the impulses of patriarchal structures and cultures that insist it is the woman's role to leave her family and join her life with the man's.

Also contradicting patriarchal tradition, the word "cleaving" in the Hebrew Bible almost always describes Israel clinging to God, the weaker to the stronger (e.g., Josh. 23:8; Ps. 91:4), but not the other way around. Years ago, I remember seeing a picture during a hard-hitting hurricane season that made the front page of many national newspapers. It showed a man desperately holding on to a lamppost while his body was whipped around and brought to a fully horizontal position. His life depended on his ability to hold on to something stronger than himself at a time of great vulnerability. From the beginning, strength and equality were implied in the role of woman as helper/partner to the man from whom she came. As creation was surveyed at each phase in chapter one, God declared that it was good, but when reviewing the creation of human beings, God called it "very good."[4] The only time something was pronounced "not good" was when the man was alone and no helper/partner had been found suitable for him. The man appears to have had no knowledge of, or participation in, the creation of the woman, yet when he awakens from the surgery, he marvels at God's handiwork and immediately recognizes her as his flesh and bone. It is their similarity that the man finds striking, not their differences.

The role of helper/partner is invaluable to the overall design of God's creation. In this context, both partners serve as co-workers. This understanding is consistent with the use of *ezer*, Hebrew for "helper," as it is used in numerous Hebrew Bible passages to describe God's help to Israel (see Exod. 18:4; Ps. 20:2; 33:20; 54:4; 70:5; 86:17; 118:13; 146:5).[5] In these passages, God helps the people by "protecting, supporting, shielding, delivering, comforting, giving hope and blessing. God's ministry of help is described in connection with action words indicating strength. Being a helper is neither a lesser role nor a weaker role. Helping is certainly not a passive role."[6] Marva Dawn further emphasizes the point when she suggests that the title of helper "contradicts a patriarchal culture by elevating woman's imaging of God, the Helper Superior. The woman is called a Helper Corresponding [*ezer kenegdo*], imaging the care of God in a human, rather than divine, way."[7] The mutuality of the helper/partner relationship between women and men is also consistent with the very character and person of God presented in three distinct persons, yet always a wholly unified one. The Trinity gives us a perfect example of difference in function but quality in existence. Likewise, even though men and women may be different in person and function, they are designed to live in mutuality, harmony, and unity.

When Eve and then Adam ate the forbidden fruit, their sin shattered the perfection of God's creation and God's intentions for it. The ripple effects of their sin are seen first in Genesis 3, but the consequences continue: Cain kills Abel (Gen. 4); God destroys the world by flood because of the prevalent wickedness (Gen. 6); the earth's population gathers to build a tower to make a name for themselves (Gen. 11); and so on. Yet in each instance, God's providential love and mercy are also evident. God expelled Adam and Eve from the Garden to keep them from eating from the tree of life and living forever in a state of separation and death. God provided clothing for them as they left, much like a mother would in caring for her children. When Cain murdered Abel, he was sent from the presence of God, but God placed a mark on him for protection. Noah and his family were saved even as God destroyed the rest of the earth. After God confused the language of humanity and dispersed the people across the face of the earth, God made a covenant with Abraham, offering hope for future generations and the promise of a new land.

The effects of sin were broad and devastating—nothing God created was unaffected. They were also close and painful—every relationship was altered. The disobedience to God's command went well beyond the simple act of eating forbidden fruit: it was a matter of intention, attitude, and relationship. Eve and Adam, unwilling to trust God completely and live in perfect relationship with their creator, chose their own desires, sought their independence, acted on their self-determination, and faced the consequences. Among other devastation, sin radically changed the relationship between Adam and Eve as man and woman; it marred the relationship with and between their children with hatred, jealousy, and even murder. The whole world, then as now, participated in the sin that was unleashed in the Garden.

God had to respond to the first humans' behavior and decisions, as God does to ours. Many of us know the pronouncements in Genesis 3 all too well. The question, however, is whether those declarations are to be taken as prescriptive or descriptive. If they are prescriptive, then the fall is still in full force today, directly affecting our lives and reflecting God's ongoing will. If they are descriptive, then what happened at Eden is still with us and yet does not reflect God's will. Understanding God's words in Genesis 3 as descriptive rather than prescriptive is consistent with what other Scriptural passages reveal about God's nature and response to sin. For example, in Exodus 20, the second commandment instructs Israel to have no other gods and not to make idols of any kind. The rationale for these commandments flows directly from God's nature: "For I the Lord your God am a jealous God, punishing children for the iniquity of parents, to the third and fourth generation of those who reject me, but showing steadfast love to the thousandth generation of those who love me and keep my commandments" (Exod. 20:5b–6; cf. also, Exod. 34:6–7, Num. 14:18, Ps. 103:8–14).

I grew up in an alcoholic home. My father, a drunk for fourteen years, sobered up when I was only two years old. From that time on he struggled to live by the principles of Alcoholics Anonymous (AA) for over forty-seven years. In second grade, I discovered that not everyone went to AA on Saturday night and church on Sunday. It is easy to speak of Dad's ongoing recovery, to acknowledge the many ways he helped others. It is far more challenging to speak of the scars that my siblings and I bear from his drinking, his selfishness, his sin. Please understand that I in no way intend to dishonor my father. In fact, I have spent much of my life also in recovery trying to become a woman whose life honors those around me, especially my family. Yet I still bear those scars, and the generations that follow may, as well.

Many of my family members share a propensity for addictive/obsessive behavior that must be surrendered to the Lord—we do not have to act upon it. The faithful witness of my father and others in the family let us know that it is possible to overcome sin. It does not have to define us or determine how we live. I know that my selfishness and sin have scarred others, and I feel that sorrow and pain. But the theological truth being revealed in the creation account is that the consequences of sin are not endless. The point of the third and fourth generation is not necessarily to formulate how long the consequences of sin will last but rather to contrast them with the blessings of faithfulness to the thousandth generation, which are forever.

In Genesis 3, God pronounced two curses—one on the ground and one on the serpent.[8] Although the first man and woman also obviously felt the effects of these curses, they were not cursed. Instead, the pronouncements of God indicate that they suffered the consequences of their sin. Unfortunately, when I survey college classes I teach about whether they grew up believing they were cursed because of the first sin, many of my female students raise their hands; few males, if any, ever do. The sense young women have of feeling cursed directly relates to their feminine identity and sexuality. The consequences God gave were gender specific. Eve would endure increased pain in childbirth and a longing for her husband. Adam would work harder and suffer in that labor, contending with the earth that is now under a curse.

Adam became subject to the soil from which he had been taken. Eve became subject to Adam from whom she had been taken . . . As a result of Satan's work, man was now master over woman, just as the mother-ground was now master over man. For these reasons it is proper to regard both male dominance and death as being antithetical to God's original intent in creation.[9]

Much attention has been given to what it means for women to have increased pain in childbirth and to have a greater desire for her husband who will rule over her. Anatomically it seems obvious that delivering a child through a narrow opening had the potential to be at least uncomfortable, quite possibly painful, even before the fall. Rather than speaking of increased physical pain of the woman in childbirth, however, I am convinced that the pain Eve experienced was grief and shame over her own sin and its effects on the lives of her children and grandchildren.[10] Giving birth to my children was physically painful, but the far greater anguish has been seeing how my unfaithfulness has hurt and damaged them.

Julia Kristeva understands the nature of the pain women suffer through childbirth. She writes, "One does not give birth in pain, one gives birth to pain: the child represents it and henceforth it settles in, it is continuous. Obviously you may close your eyes, cover up your ears, teach courses, run errands, tidy up the house, think about objects, subjects. But a mother is always branded by pain, she yields to it."[11] Likewise, the desire that Eve felt toward her husband, who would now rule over her, also has been greatly misunderstood. God does not seem to be describing a sexual desire that Eve would have for Adam, an emotional longing for her husband's companionship when he was away at work, or a vengeful wish to dominate him instead of being dominated (all three interpretations offered by contemporary scholars). Rather Eve's longing, I believe, appears to be one of sorrow and regret that her sin and Adam's had distorted the mutual, harmonious, and unified wholeness of the relationship God intended for them. Understandably, she longed for what she had once had and was unlikely to gain again with her husband.

Adam, on the other hand, was destined to till the ground in hard labor. Not only did the sin of the first man and woman cause their expulsion from the beautiful garden God gave them, a place where work would be required but not onerous, but it also disrupted the nature of their God-intended relationship: "The ruler/subject relationship between Adam and Eve began after the fall. It was for Eve the application of the same death principle that made Adam slave to the soil. Because it resulted from the fall, the rule of Adam over Eve is viewed as satanic in origin, no less than is death itself."[12] Equally devastating is the fact that the two sons who naturally would have toiled with him were gone as a result of sin. Anyone growing up in a farming community knows the importance of having strong sons to work the fields, a job too large for just one person. But Adam's sons were both gone: he lost one to death and the other to exile. He was alone and I am confident that each time he tilled the soil, he was reminded not only where he came from but also how terribly he messed it all up. As in the rest of Genesis, Adam and Eve felt the effects of their sin in their relationships with God, each other, their offspring, and future generations.

But as faithful people believe, sin never has the last word. Even as God punished Adam's and Eve's sin and delineated the results, God still acted with characteristic redemption and mercy. When God pronounced judgment for the woman's sin, God also offered hope by relating redemption to motherhood:

> The woman's offspring will crush the serpent who is the embodiment of evil . . . The three aspects of this redemptive motherhood revealed in the account of God's response to the sinful disobedience of the man and woman are characteristic of the overall biblical paradigm for prophetic ministry: struggle, suffering and servanthood.[13]

Enmity between the serpent and woman were characteristic of the classic struggles between good and evil, life and death. Through the painful process of giving birth, the woman would suffer yet also offer hope for the eventual birth of the redeemer.

And finally, even though the effects of Adam and Eve's sin were felt for several generations within their lifetimes, God offered them immediate hope of renewed life in their ancestral lineage. At the birth of Seth (Gen. 4:25), Adam recognized that it was God who had given him another son. The sin of Adam and Eve, like all sin we commit, had consequences felt for three or four generations but not necessarily beyond. With Enosh, Seth's son, people began "to call upon the name of the Lord" (4:26). From the beginning God placed limits on the dominion of sin but not on the blessings received by those who lived in love and faithfulness. God's steadfast love is promised endlessly to those "who love and keep my commandments" (see Exod. 20:5b–6).

Thoughts on Working Together

"I started the semester with the idea that a partnership was just being really good friends that work together. In this situation we did become friends, but the partnership we gained was not just becoming friends. I thought that partnership was a function of a friendship. While this is somewhat true, it's more than that. Partnership develops when we are intentionally open with one another, when we make things work, when we deliberately set aside differences to reach a common goal, and when we force ourselves to be accountable to each other. A godly partnership develops when we are deliberate and intentional about observing spiritual discipline in all areas."

—Male Student

Clearly the beginning of humanity was filled with contrast and intrigue—beauty and harmony, sin and despair, hope and recommitment. The witness throughout the rest of the Hebrew Bible is one of continuous disharmony, disunity, and sin, and the resulting consequences suffered by the unfaithful. It is also, however, a testimony of great godly men and women who powerfully influenced the lives of those around them. God's design for partnership between men and women is evident in the creation narrative even after the barrier of sin enters. The question faced by men and women, then and now, is whether they chose (or will choose) to accept the model of godly partnership or continue sinning against God and one another?

The Narrative of the Hebrew Bible

Another key story about partnership in the Old Testament begins with the Lord calling Abraham to leave his country and his father's household and journey to a land that God would provide. God promised not only that Abraham's name would be honored and that a great nation would be built through him, but also that all the nations of the earth would be blessed. Faithfully, Abraham, at age seventy-five, responded by taking his wife Sarah, his nephew Lot, and all of their possessions and people, and setting out on this remarkable trek. The narrative that follows crosses several countries and numerous generations. It is full of tales of mistrust, deception, and betrayal as well as faithfulness, hope, and redemption—all qualities of any bestseller today. Those of us well-versed in Scripture could probably tell the story without much thought. In this section, I want to focus primarily on the partnership that existed between Abraham and Sarah.

When God called them out of their comfortable lives and into this journey, both Abraham and Sarah were well advanced in years, beyond what any obstetrician or fertility expert would expect to support childbearing. Scripture simply states, "Now Sarai was barren; she had no children"

(Gen. 11:30). Yet the covenant was contingent on a child being born from this union, and Abraham and Sarah proceeded believing that God would fulfill what was promised. Sometimes I think we miss how utterly ridiculous this story really is and how difficult it must have been to believe God's promise.

Years ago, Jack and I were teaching at a camp for fourth through eighth graders. Both of our girls were campers, and our then five-year-old son Jay stayed with us too, participating on the sidelines. Jack's assignment was to teach the story of Abraham, Sarah, and Isaac. He struggled to think of a creative way to retell the familiar story, particularly in the distracting circumstances of camp. He began the session by talking to the children about what they especially loved about their grandparents. Jack told stories of visiting his grandmother, Mama Muns, and how much he loved going to her house, climbing trees, visiting the dime store, and playing with cousins. Jack related that recently Mama, then in her early 90s, had not been feeling well, that her stomach kept hurting. His mother took Mama to the doctor hoping that it was nothing serious. He related how surprised both his mother and grandmother were with the diagnosis: Mama Muns was pregnant! All of the children gasped, but the look on Jay's face was priceless. Of course, Jack made it clear to the campers that this was just an illustration to help them understand the biblical story, but it took us days to explain to Jay that Mama really wasn't pregnant and why his Dad had said something that wasn't true.

The story of Abraham and Sarah is just that farfetched and difficult to comprehend. We like to tell it as if it is one of great faith and trust in God, and it is. But it is also a story with twists and turns that cannot be ignored. Twice Abraham passed Sarah off as his sister (a partial truth since they were half-siblings sharing the same father) to save his life (cf. Gen. 12:10–20; 20).[14] Apparently Sarah was a beautiful and desirable woman at sixty-five and even in her late eighties—something many of us hope for but know we will not attain.

On two different occasions both Abraham and Sarah laughed at the audacity of having a child at their advanced ages (Gen. 17:17 and 18:12–15). Each of them sought a solution to "help God out" in fulfilling what was obviously taking too long. Early on Abraham tried to name one of his servants as an heir (Gen. 15:1–6), and Sarah led her husband to conceive a child with her maidservant, Hagar (Gen. 16:1–6). The latter had devastating consequences for all concerned. But God's purpose and plan were not deterred by their actions. Like many of us, Abraham and Sarah failed to trust God's promises as individuals but especially as partners.

Abraham and Sarah finally conceived and gave birth to Isaac. And barrenness, cunning, deceit, and contention continued to surface in their family lineage right alongside faithfulness, trust, hope, and blessing.[15] God used Abraham and Sarah, Isaac and Rebekah, Jacob and Rachel to continually unfold the promises made and to use their partnerships in the process. Just as Adam and Eve's sin affected their children to the third or fourth generation, so did Abraham and Sarah's. With the fourth generation, however, just as Enosh began to follow the Lord, God once again was able to live in and bless Joseph even in the midst of particularly trying circumstances (see Gen. 37–50). These collective stories give us hope that even in our failures, our mistrust, and our sin, God is still very much at work forming us into meaningful partners to fulfill covenant promises.

Stories of other strong marriage partnerships can be found throughout the Old Testament. Hannah suffered from barrenness. Her loving husband, Elkanah, gave her double portions of the sacrifice to be offered with their prayers in hope that God would open her womb (1 Sam. 1:3–11). The result of their union was the great prophet Samuel. The Moabite Ruth, ancestor to David and eventually Jesus, served as the breadwinner of her family by gleaning in the fields. Ruth eventually married her kinsman Boaz and through her lineage the Messiah was born. The Song of Songs abounds with expressions of mutual relationship and high esteem. But godly partnerships were not limited to marriage.

God chose Moses to deliver the people from bondage in Egypt and to form them into a covenant people. Yet often we fail to see the numerous partnerships that served God's purpose in Moses' life. Miriam, Moses' sister, was a faithful partner to her brother as she watched over him hidden in the river. His adoptive mother, Pharoah's daughter, saved the newborn infant from death decreed by her father. Miriam ensured his well-being by providing their mother as his nursemaid (Exod. 2:1–10). As God called Moses at the burning bush, Aaron, Moses' brother, was already on his way to assist Moses in the challenges ahead (Exod. 4:14–17). Miriam, now identified as a prophetess, joined Moses in singing of God's deliverance at the parting of the Red Sea and she led the women in singing and dancing to further glorify the Lord (Gen. 15:1–21).

Any of us with brothers or sisters can imagine that these sibling partnerships were not without trouble. When Moses went up Sinai to receive the tablets of stone on which God wrote the Law, Aaron was unable to withstand the pleas of the people. He assisted them in building an idol and altar upon which to worship it, thereby incurring God's wrath (Gen. 32:1–33:6). In another incident, Aaron and Miriam criticized Moses' leadership and angered the Lord. As a result, Miriam contracted leprosy and both brothers pleaded for her deliverance (Num. 12); she only suffered a week away from the people before she was completely healed.

Other interesting partnerships are found throughout Israel's history. Deborah served as a deliverer in Israel and was named as a prophet and judge (Judg. 4–5). As such, she settled disputes and served as a military leader. When she called Barak to lead an assault against Israel's enemies, he agreed to go only if she accompanied him—and their partnership resulted in victory for Israel. Esther stands out as a national figure whose bravery and fortitude served God's purposes and people well. Her partnership with her cousin, Mordecai, saved Israel from certain destruction. It is because of their work that the Purim holiday is celebrated even today.

Thoughts on Working Together

"From these last few months I have seen that although it is not solely my responsibility on the team to fix or challenge everything, it is my responsibility to call out weaknesses or areas that I see need to be fixed, [so they can be] brought to the surface and dealt with, even if that means the discussion itself is the only result. Beyond that, I cannot change the way people behave or the way they think; that is up to God. But I can bring myself to the table, willing to learn, willing to change, and giving my best effort to contribute to the team and make the process more beneficial for everyone involved."

—Female Student

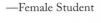

Too often we hear these stories only as indications of strong women being used by God and fail to see the unusual and meaningful partnerships they formed to strengthen and encourage them in their calling. God's design for partnership between men and women was realized even though sin and its consequences remained pervasive. From the patriarchs to the judges, from the kings to the prophets, the people failed to trust their faithful God. Yet hope was never completely lost. Throughout their history, God's people remembered past deliverance and relied on fulfilled promises. A new day was coming. On the "Day of the Lord," whole new partnerships would be formed and God's purposes realized through them: "I will pour out my Spirit on all people. Your sons and daughters will prophesy, your old men will dream dreams, your young men will see visions. Even on my servants, both men and women, I will pour out my Spirit in those days" (Joel 2:28–29). The people knew to anticipate something revolutionary and transformational, but the realization of this promise would be well beyond what anyone could imagine.

The New Order in the New Testament

A poor teenager. A woman without status or privilege. A virgin betrothed to an older man. This woman, not another, is God's choice as a partner in bringing Jesus to earth. The prophetic word given Eve in Genesis 3 is fulfilled. The story is unbelievable and outrageous, and yet it is the beginning of the gospel and a story upon which many of us stake our lives. God became human, lived among us, and eventually gave up that life in a hideous death. Through the resurrection, Jesus offers hope for a new life, realization of God's original design, fulfillment of all God's promises, and the formation of a new people.

Paul writes to the Corinthian church reminding them that ". . . if anyone is in Christ, there is a new creation: everything old has passed away; see everything has become new!" (2 Cor. 5:7). The Gospel of Matthew clearly states that Jesus came to fulfill all the law and prophets, to bring the covenants of God to completion (5:17–20). Clearly God is also forming a new people: "[b]ut you are a chosen race, a royal priesthood, a holy nation, God's own people in order that you may proclaim the mighty acts of the one who called you out of darkness into his marvelous light" (1 Pet. 2:9).

Luke describes what happens to the first Christians as they are formed into the new Israel,

> Awe came upon everyone, because many wonders and signs were being done by the apostles: All who believed were together and had all things in common. . . . Day by day, as they spent much time together in the temple, they broke bread at home and ate their food with glad and generous hearts, praising God and having the goodwill of all the people. (Acts 2:43–47b)

Pentecost marked a critical moment in church history, dramatically revealing that *everyone* is welcome into the community of faith.[16] All believers have equal standing and are called to be new creatures in Christ who serve as ambassadors in the Kingdom.[17] Groothius notes,

> In the new covenant, God shows no favoritism for one group of people over another (Acts 10:34–35; Romans 2:11; James 2:8–9), and believers are filled with the Holy Spirit and gifted in prophetic ministry without respect to age, gender, or social status (Acts 2:17–18). According to Galatians 3:26–28, all believers are "sons," or heirs, in Christ; there is no longer any distinction in spiritual privilege or status between either Jew or Gentile, slave or free, male or female. First Peter 3:7 states that husband and wife are equal heirs of God's gift of life, and Romans 8:15–17 declares that all believers are adopted sons of God and hence "heirs of God and co-heirs with Christ."[18]

The mutuality, harmony, and unity of relationships experienced by the first believers reflect the beauty of God's original design, the joy of life lived in Jesus Christ, and the transforming power available to all believers through the Holy Spirit.

All of the Gospels, but particularly Luke and Acts, serve as unique testimonies of the significant roles women played as helpers, leaders, and partners alongside their Christian brothers in the coming of the Kingdom. The Pauline epistles highlight women's participation with men in the establishment of and service to the church. Women are named in virtually every ministry (the exception is *overseer/elder*, but men were not identified specifically by name in these roles either), something unparalleled in the ancient world. Women served as teachers, apostles, deaconesses, patronesses, prophets, evangelists, worship leaders, and ministering widows.[19] Examples of the valuable contributions of partnerships between men and women abound in the New Testament, but I will mention a few here for emphasis.

Several women are noticeably significant partners in Jesus' life and ministry. Mary Magdalene, Joanna, Susanna, and others served as patronesses for the ministry of Jesus and the disciples, not only underwriting but also traveling with them (Luke 8:1–3). Two sisters, Mary and Martha, plus their brother, Lazarus, opened their home to Jesus and served their friend in very personal and meaningful ways. Jesus enters this sibling relationship between sisters and uses it to instruct Martha on what is most important in a life of faith—sitting at the feet of the master (Luke 10:38–42). In a confrontation after the death of her brother, Martha declared her faith in Jesus as the Messiah (John 11:24–26) just as Peter had earlier (John 6:66–71).

In another incident Jesus commended a poor widow to the disciples for her faithfulness and generosity as she gave two coins, all that she had, at the temple (Luke 21:1-4). Women were the last at the cross and the first at the tomb, and they proclaimed the good news that Jesus had risen to the eleven surviving apostles and others (Luke 23:55–56, 24:1–10).

After Pentecost, men and women continued to serve together in the advancement of the faith. Interestingly, Paul is often thought of as advocating the subjugation of women, yet in each of these passages, he clearly formed a valued partnership with numerous Christian sisters. Tabitha served a group of widows and orphans, and they were so bereft at her death that Paul was compelled to bring her back so that she could continue in her good works (Acts 9:36–42). Lydia, a wealthy merchant and head of her household, engaged in perhaps the first documented women's ministry as she gathered with other God-fearers in Philippi. She met Paul, and upon hearing the gospel, she and her whole household were baptized, thus forming the first church in that area (Acts 16:11–15, 40).

Priscilla and Aquila taught Apollos and continued to serve as co-workers and co-leaders with Paul and each other (Acts 18:24–28). Philip the evangelist had four unmarried daughters who prophesied (Acts 21:8–9). The apostle Paul and the church in Rome valued the service rendered by Phoebe, a commended deaconess, and Junia is mentioned as prominent among the apostles (Rom. 16:1, 7). Other women highly valued by Paul were Euodia and Syntyche from Philippi who, though they were in some sort of disagreement, obviously made significant contributions to ministry (Phil. 4:2–3). And finally, Lois and Eunice were noted by Paul as women whose godly influence shaped the character and faith of their son and grandson, whom Paul claimed as his spiritual son, Timothy (2 Tim. 1:5).

The emphasis in all these passages is on faithfulness, unity, surrender, discipleship, mission, blessing, giving, serving, learning, healing, sharing, giftedness, honoring, teaching, partnership, mutuality, and prayer—all characteristics of God's reign on earth. The first Christians experienced the transforming power of Jesus yet also lived in anticipation of even greater fullness when Christ would come again:

> Our Lord liberated men and women from their bondage to the social orders that violate God's intention for human life-in-community. Jesus freed males from the role of domination that belongs to the fallen world, in order that they can be truly male. On behalf of women Jesus acted as the model human standing against the patriarchal system, bringing women into the new order where sex distinctions no longer determine rank and worth.[20]

Yet this new paradigm has not always been realized. From mainline Protestant churches to obscure fundamentalist groups, from Roman Catholics to Pentecostals, Christians for the past two thousand years have dealt with men and women of all ages, classes, and ethnicities who struggle with issues of the new order. Ruth Tucker and Walter L. Liefeld examine church history from a woman's perspective with insightful results. They identify several discernable patterns and trends that signify the continual struggle throughout the history of Christianity over issues of mutuality, harmony, and unity—all of which affect the formation of godly partnership. Among their notes are the following:

- Women were very prominent in church history. The history of religion is probably the only field of history where women have had such an influential role—even though they were systematically denied positions of authority.
- Women often had significant leadership positions during the initial pioneering and developmental stages of a movement, only to be replaced by men as the movement became more "respectable."
- Throughout the history of the church, different views about women have coexisted within the same culture of religion. It is incorrect to assume that leaders or representatives of a particular movement (e.g., the ancient Jewish rabbis) had a monolithic understanding of women.
- Women have been very active in a wide variety of ministries within the institutionalized church despite pronouncements and official decrees to the contrary.
- A personal religious "call" (sometimes accompanied by visions or trances) has been an important factor in justifying ministry for women, as it has been for justifying the ministry of lay men who sought preaching roles in the church.
- Women appear to have been far more concerned with social needs and the unity of the believers than with doctrinal issues—particularly the "nonessentials" of the Christian creed. Women have, in fact, had a significant influence on ecumenical activities in the church.[21]

Tucker and Liefeld also dispel a number of popularly held assumptions or myths regarding women in the church. They found that the churches labeled "liberal" have not always been more open to the ministry of women than the so-called conservative churches have been consistently closed to it. Neither did they find that women historically have been more easily deceived than men, nor are they more often the founder of cults and authors of heresies—all accusations often leveled at women throughout Christian history. They find unsubstantiated the charge that women are more emotionally inclined than men and turn more often to sectarian, ecstatic religions in larger numbers. Finally, they offer a significant insight that deserves particular attention in a discussion on partnership:

> One of the most widely held views on women in the church—and particularly on those in leadership positions—is that they have manifested a feminist impulse. Both feminists and traditionalists have lent their support to this view. To the contrary, however, we have found that women seemed very hesitant to challenge the "rightful" leadership of men. Rarely did they manifest purely feminist qualities; rather, they were cautious about seeking a place of prominence in the church. When they did strive for positions in ministry, their motivation appeared to be to serve more effectively.[22]

Even more ironic than the fact that these issues have plagued the church for the last two millennia is the fact that the difficulties initially arose in Pauline churches. Paul, with whom numerous godly partnerships were formed and utilized, corrected two unfortunate instances of women's misconduct in worship especially as it related to their husbands. He instructed the women in Corinth who were praying and prophesying with their heads uncovered to conduct themselves with greater propriety. They needed to cover their heads (1 Cor. 11:3–16). Later in the same epistle, he instructed wives who were publicly correcting their husbands in the assembly to be quiet (1 Cor. 14:33–40). The church in Ephesus had been the target of false teachers, and the witness of the church was threatened by misconduct on several fronts. Paul wrote specifically to the women there about how they were to dress, how they should learn, and how they ought to live holy lives that reflected their salvation (1 Tim. 2:11–15).

In most discussions about gender issues in Christian ministry, these three texts become the primary focal point, and serious attempts are made to exegete and interpret them properly. Careful and faithful exegesis, however, has not always led to a clear-cut interpretation upon which most Christians could agree (see the proliferation of works on this single topic in any Christian bookstore). Although discussions on women's roles in worship and ministry are significant and should be conducted within the church, attention should also focus on how women and men might serve together as co-workers in godly partnerships. Scripture is full of such relationships, and it is clear that they were intended to be the norm of our life in the Lord.

Thoughts on Working Together

"As I have experienced and studied group dynamics and ministry, I have been able to see how many diverse gifts God has given people. Nobody is gifted in enough ways to effectively minister without others, and some people are gifted more than others in different areas. Obviously, God has designed us for partnership. By gifting his people in numerous ways, God has created us to work better together."

—Male Student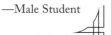

Partnership does not happen simply because we are Christians. When the women announced Jesus' resurrection, the disciples dismissed the news as idle talk and did not believe them. Just as the first disciples failed to believe those women, so too we often fail to listen to and understand one another. Just as differences grew up among the earliest believers over cultural and social boundaries, so too we continue in similar conflicts today. Just as gender issues threatened the unity of the early church and the individuals in it, so too are we confused and challenged as we share life together. But these failures, conflicts, and threats are not the last word on godly partnership. The last word belongs to God. It belongs to God who lives in partnership within the Trinity in perfect love, harmony, honor, and unity. It belongs to God who calls each of us, and all of us, to live in meaningful relationship with God's self. It belongs to God who places us in numerous situations that we share as men and women. To fulfill what God intends for us, we must learn to be together in new and meaningful ways. To do so we are called to a deeper surrender, to live continually in a position of yielding. The next chapter is devoted to helping us see exactly what that looks like in our relationships as men and women in the Lord.

Conclusion

Eleven years have passed since I stood in prayer with my male colleagues in the classroom. The partnerships God forged in our lives have been at once meaningful and challenging. Each one taught us something about ourselves but also about each other. We learned to work more closely, more effectively, and I think more faithfully as women and men. Looking back I know that I am a different person, a better one, because of my male friends and colleagues.

Eventually what we experienced together led us to set up learning experiences through which our students could explore their partnerships as men and women. I will develop more about those learning activities in Chapter Three. Other experiences, however, have also shaped my understanding of and experience with partnership. In Chapter Two, I describe one particularly significant event that continues to challenge my thinking about and participation in partnerships.

Notes to Chapter One

1. The contents of this chapter were first published as "Co-Workers in the Lord: A Theology of Partnership for Men and Women in Ministry/Missions," a Festschrift for Ian Fair, *Restoration Quarterly,* Vol. 45/Numbers 1 and 2, First and Second Quarters 2003, 106–14. Permission has been granted for use here, and the material has been adapted for inclusion in this book.
2. Mary Stewart Van Leeuwen, *Gender and Grace: Love, Work and Parenting in a Changing World* (Downers Grove: InterVarsity, 1990), 110.
3. Rick R. Marrs, *Embracing the Call of God: Finding Ourselves in Genesis* (Webb City, MO: Covenant, 2003), 47.
4. God's declaration of the goodness of creation is not a moral designation but a functional observation that what has been made fits perfectly with God's intention for it and affirms both God's dominion over creation and creation's subordination and dependence on God. As Rick Marrs writes, "Even the heavenly bodies are not independent of God, but stand in his service (designating the seasons and separating day and night)" (*Embracing* 29). God's sovereignty is implicit from the beginning. In creating humanity on the sixth day and resting on the seventh, three features of the narrative further underscore God's reign:
   a) The plural language of Genesis 1:26, "let us make humankind in our image," is often falsely interpreted as Trinitarian—a designation that would not have been understood or relevant to the original audience. Rather the scene, according to Marrs, is one of God surrounded by a divine council "as [an] omnipotent monarch seated on a throne and surrounded by divine beings . . ." who will faithfully do the king's bidding (30). Such a picture of God as king is common in the Old Testament (see for examples 1 Kings 22; Psalm 82; Job 1–2, Isaiah 6).
   b) This understanding of God's reign is indicated also by the creation of humanity, both male and female, in the image of God. Conquering kings in the Ancient Near East mapped out the conquered lands and established sovereignty by erecting statues of their images for the people to observe. Rather than erecting such a statue, God "bestows royalty upon his created subjects . . . [and]

God's image carries no socio-economic, ethnic or gender distinctions" (31).

c) Furthermore, a common inscription under these statues indicated that the king rested over the conquered land and people. When God rests on the seventh day and sanctifies the Sabbath, there is a complete picture of God's sovereignty and peace over all that has been created.

5. Susan Hunt and Peggy Hutcheson, *Leadership for Women in the Church* (Grand Rapids: Zondervan, 1991), 28.

6. Ibid., 29.

7. Marva J. Dawn, *Reaching Out without Dumbing Down* (Grand Rapids: Eerdmans, 1995), 100.

8. Gerhard von Rad, *Genesis: A Commentary*, trans. John H. Marks (Philadelphia: Westminster, 1961), 90.

9. Gilbert Bilezikian, *Beyond Sex Roles: What the Bible Says about a Women's Place in Church and Family* (Grand Rapids: Baker, 1985), 49. Also relevant here is the work of Claus Westermann, who sees these pronouncements by God as descriptions of the difficulties of life as it would be lived now between Adam and Eve. He states, ". . . the clause in Genesis 3:16 expresses only one side of the relationship of man and woman, whereas in 2:21–24 man and woman are equals, and no trace of subordination is to be found. In contrast to the temporary subordination of the woman stands the permanent relationship between man and woman: the difference between them is a part of human existence that will always remain." Claus Westermann, *Genesis: A Practical Commentary*, trans. David E. Green (Grand Rapids: Eerdmans, 1987), 26.

10. Neither of the Hebrew words normally used to describe pain in childbirth is used in the Genesis 3 passage. Gordon J. Wenham, "Genesis 1-15," *Word Biblical Commentary*, Vol. 1 (Waco: Word, 1987), 81.

11. Julia Kristeva, "Stabat Mater," *Contemporary Literary Criticism: Literary and Cultural Studies,* 2nd edition, eds. Robert Con Davis and Ronald Schleifer (New York: Longman, 1989), 190.

12. Bilezikian, 58.

13. Cheryl J. Sanders, *Ministry at the Margins: The Prophetic Mission of Women, Youth and the Poor* (Downers Grove: InterVarsity, 1997), 46.

14. In the first instance the text seems to imply that the Pharaoh of Egypt took Sarai as his wife; in the second she seems to be spared this indignity.

15. Compare the Genesis accounts of the patriarchs (Gen. 24–37) with how they are viewed in Hebrews 11.
16. Prior to Pentecost, circumcision for males was the sign of the covenant. After Pentecost, baptism, open to everyone, is the sign of the new covenant.
17. For insight into the relationship between Pentecost and gender in Christianity, see Gretchen Gaebelein Hull, *Equal to Serve: Women and Men Working Together Revealing the Gospel* (Grand Rapids: Baker, 1998), 66.
18. Rebecca Merrill Groothius, *Good News for Women: A Biblical Picture of Gender Equality* (Grand Rapids: Baker, 1997), 20.
19. Linda L. Belleville, *Women Leaders and the Church: Three Crucial Questions* (Grand Rapids: Baker, 2000), 50–69.
20. Stanley J. Grenz with Denise Muir Kjesbo, *Women in the Church: A Biblical Theology of Women in Ministry* (Downers Grove: InterVarsity, 1995), 209.
21. Ruth Tucker and Walter L. Liefeld, *Daughters of the Church: From New Testament Times to the Present* (Grand Rapids: Zondervan, 1987), 14–15.
22. Ibid., 16.

Chapter Two

A Call to Repent and Reclaim

Where We Need to Pay Attention

Four of us women, two black and two white, were asked to address the New Wineskins retreat, a gathering of mostly African American preachers, all males. The men's question to us had been, what do men in the church need to hear from women in order to serve more effectively? Each of us had prayed, prepared, and corresponded with one another, and so our first face-to-face meeting was rich and engaging. Sharing from our lives and ministries, it was obvious that this experience was not only a significant historical event but also a deeply personal one. All of us agreed if we had come for nothing more than the conversation together, the trip was worth it.

Yet there was so much more in store for all of us.

Because my subject was a theology of partnership that began in Genesis, we decided I would go first. I felt confident about the material I had prepared but not about the presentation. The leaders of the gathering asked that it be biblical, even theological, but not scholarly. They wanted it to "preach."

That night I was going over my notes, praying over the contents, and struggling to find a suitable conclusion. After about an hour of wrestling with it, I shared my dilemma with my husband Jack. He asked me one simple question—what did I hope would change because of that presentation? My response was swift, immediate, and passionate. He grabbed a pen and paper and began to quickly write down what I said.

I had the conclusion of the presentation completed but trembled at the thought of sharing it with others. I still do.

Defining partnership between men and women would seem to be a simple enough task, and yet formulating such a definition is as complicated and challenging as any relationship between the sexes. Among the questions that come to mind: Which men and women are trying to form relationship? What is the basis for it? Why is partnership important to our functioning together? What is the partnership for? How do we discover its purpose? How will we know if it is working or not? In defining partnership for this discussion, I am indebted to Ruth Haley Barton in her book, *Equal to the Task.* Her work has been meaningful to me both in the classroom and in my life. She defines partnership as a "journey of the heart . . . [into] an unknown, an opening to a transforming power that we have rarely experienced. It is the admission that before men and women can *accomplish* things together, we must learn *to be together* in love, in compassion, in truth, in body, in strength, in vulnerability—in God."[1]

Some Basic Assumptions

Understanding Barton's definition and realizing it in our partnerships means that we must look at what lies behind it from a Christian perspective. Women and men, reflecting the image of God in which we were created, are meant by God's design to work in harmonious, mutual, and unified partnership with one another. This understanding is the norm that should govern male and female relationships in all dimensions of community life—marriage, friendship, volunteer work, and professional relationships. Even though we acknowledge that sin marred the original creation, and still does, we also know that God made provision in both the Hebrew Bible and the New Testament, especially in Jesus Christ, for God's people to reclaim the blessing of our partnerships. God's redemptive nature has been and will be at work among Christians to accomplish and enhance God's purposes in all our relationships. Part of reclaiming godly partnership, however, entails making concerted efforts to have men and women working together in many contexts.

Yet there are unique challenges we face as we forge new partnerships and live within existing ones. These challenges must be met forthrightly and diligently to avoid diminishing our Christian witness. Although sexual matters are difficult to address without embarrassment or misunderstanding, true partnership can only happen in mixed-gender groups when people openly address the issues. Avoiding contact with the opposite sex or failure to have open discussions only drive these delicate issues underground and make them more difficult for the community of faith to handle.[2] I agree with Sarah Sumner, who thinks "it should be normal for people in the church to fight together for sexual purity. Most of the time the subject is so taboo that we feel way too ashamed to admit our temptations, much less to confess our sin."[3]

A youth minister mentioned to me one day that he was astounded that Jack and I both taught our children about their sexuality, even the difficult issues of masturbation, pornography, and birth control. Admittedly, I was more candid with our daughters, and Jack with our son, yet we both shared in the conversation about what it means to be male and female. Our logic was, if our kids couldn't talk to us as loving parents with whom they had grown up about important issues, how would they be able to discuss such things with their future spouses? As members of the family, we were not afraid to talk to one another even when it was difficult. But many children and adults do not have Christian parents or trusted friends to talk with about difficult issues, and here especially, the church should fill the void, as we are God's family to one another.

Do we need to exercise care as we partner on delicate topics? *Of course.* But we should not fear standing together and helping one another. At the same time, we all should repent of the way we sometimes use our bodies as instruments of lust, seduction, and temptation instead of modesty, humility, and godliness. We must call each other to high standards of faithfulness as we develop principles that guide godly partnership.

Most of these principles can and should be derived from theological reflection on Scripture, through examination of our many partnerships and how they function according to God's intention, and through the witness of great men and women of faith who have served and worked together in the past. The temptation at this point is to move immediately toward discussing the principles and characteristics that are necessary for godly partnership to be formed and sustained. But something else must happen prior to the development of these principles.

My experience in addressing the question posed by my African American brothers helped me to see that the vital first step in all our relationships is repentance. Before we can truly participate in the life that God intended for us as men and women to have together, we must repent. For what or from what must we repent? We must repent of the many thoughts, attitudes, words, and actions that divide us and allow us to feel justified in those divisions. We must examine closely not only who we are but also how we are in relationship to one another.

Only after our genuine repentance will we be free to reclaim the rightful partnership that God designed and intended for us to live out. I felt nervous as I prepared to speak to my brothers about what they needed to hear from us, their Christian sisters. I feel nervous as I write these words, but I believe all of us who live in Jesus must consider these messages. I am confident that as you read, you will discover areas where repentance is needed that I have not considered here. I am equally confident that others will find ways to reclaim what God designed and intended for us that are not addressed in this book. Whatever the outcome, my prayer is that we all will be blessed by this call to repentance and reclaiming.

Thoughts on Working Together

"From my experience and reflection on working in service-learning with my partners, I have come to learn that it is crucial to consider the people you are working with. Partnership is not about individuals who happen to have the same goal; each person involved in working out that goal has influence on the others in the group. Working for God's kingdom draws us together in communion. Availability is essential for partnership to be realized and effective. . . . I felt a greater sense of accomplishing partnership when our interest in each other grew to where we wanted to spend time together beyond our obligation to our project."

—Female Student

A Call to Christian Women

Since I am a woman, I will call any woman reading this book to prayerfully consider the following areas that I have seen present in the lives of Christian women, including my own. I hope to do so with a direct, respectful, but above all, confessional tone.

Women must repent of our participation in the current climate of misandry, the hatred or demeaning of men, that is so prevalent in our culture. Television commercials and programs, movies, literature, sermons, jokes, and stories abound that portray men as moronic, incapable of thinking well, and acting more like children than adults. I remember first becoming aware of this tendency when our son Jay was in the eighth grade. He came to the car one day obviously frustrated and angry. When I asked what was bothering him, he told me about an incident in the lunchroom that day. Apparently a group of girls had accused Jay and his friends of being "chauvinist pigs" because of something they had said in jest. Jay admitted that the teasing was inappropriate but then asked me why it was okay for the girls to feel perfectly free to say all kinds of derogatory remarks to the boys.

Jay was right. Women in our society do feel much freer to put men down and are quite intolerant of the reverse. It almost seems politically correct to demean men at any time and in almost any fashion. Media tells us that men think only about sex, food, and football (or whatever sport of their choice), that they are incapable of taking care of themselves, that they really need our constant help (translation: supervision), and whether conscientiously or not, we too often believe these messages. As Christian women we must repent of these tendencies and commit to not participating in them under any circumstances if we are to build mature relationships with our Christian brothers.

Faithful women who desire to grow in their partnerships with men should repent of the disrespect so often displayed toward men because they don't think, act, and feel like women. We often play into long-held stereotypes that women function best in certain ways and men in others. I have seen a "knowing glance" pass between women far too frequently and heard too many critical conversations among them when men do not seem to understand what is going on and we think they should. We love to talk about how "clueless" they are, how helpless and forgetful. Yes, it is frustrating that men and women do not always see or do things the same way but that is no excuse for putting the other down. Yet it is easy to fall into such attitudes and actions without even being aware that we are doing so.

Several years ago, I was overcommitted and working under especially stressful conditions—a new job, graduate classes, three children, housework, and a video project. Obviously it was too much and so my husband, Jack, who has been an equal partner in most areas, agreed to take on even more responsibility.

On a couple of nights, I returned home very late to find the kitchen immaculate—all, that is, except for the pots and pans. They were sitting on the stovetop just as they had been after dinner. When I talked to Jack about it he admitted that he just didn't see them. Several days later after a similar experience, I said to him, "You know what I need from you right now?" "No, what?" he asked, willing to help in any way. "I really need you to be another woman. I need you to see what I see and do things the way I would do them," I said, half joking, half serious. Jack looked at me and laughed, "You know, Babe, that's the one thing I'm never going to be for you." We shared another laugh about it and went to bed, leaving the dishes to soak until the next morning.

Jack is right, he will never be another woman, and I would not want him to be even if that were possible. But why did I demean him by framing the dilemma we faced this way? Instead of laughing about it, I should have apologized. This incident ended well with both of us in good humor but that is not always the case. Too often, I have felt and expressed frustration at my husband, colleagues, and friends for their lack of understanding or ability "to get it." When I did not feel that it was wise to express such things, I have often harbored them as little nuggets of frustration that had the potential to become larger stones in my heart. One little stone added to another eventually adds up to a hardheartedness that is foreign to the nature of Jesus Christ. We cannot afford to let disrespect and dishonor of men take hold in any form but must remove these pebbles, stones, and boulders before they become too heavy to manage.

At the same time Christian women must also consider how we practice misogyny, the hatred or demeaning of women. Disrespecting women damages individuals and limits our partnership with both genders. On the simplest level are women who compare themselves with other women or who make derogatory remarks about them that feed into common stereotypes. These practices are harmful to self and to all involved. On a more serious scale are women who report that they do not like being with other women, they prefer only the company of men. Early in my life I held this same sentiment until I realized that I was prejudiced against my own gender. How could I expect others to take me seriously as a woman if I refused to do the same for my sisters? Even more troubling is the propensity of some Christian women to restrict themselves and other women to a limited set of roles, insisting that they "know their place." These tendencies keep in check the use of spiritual giftedness and fail to even consider how they isolate single women in our churches. We must stop these negative practices and embrace other women as sisters and friends.

Christian women also must repent of a common misunderstanding of male headship and female submission. "All I want," I hear from many young Christian women, "is to find a man to be my spiritual head." When I probe what they mean by spiritual head they usually describe a man who can lead them for the rest of their lives. He will surely be stronger, more mature, wiser, and godlier than they are since he will be the primary breadwinner, protector, and decision-maker. These women are following misguided teachings that they have received in their homes and churches. The young men that they form friendships with, date, and sometimes marry cannot possibly fill these tall orders, and so the relationship begins on false pretenses.

A young man may have the potential to be very strong, mature, wise, and godly, but my observations tell me that he will mostly likely not begin realizing these qualities until he is at least in his thirties. So a man married to a woman with unrealistic expectations for his development soon learns to fake it and live off his potential, to give up and stay an arrested adolescent, or to go underground and seek comfort and companionship elsewhere.

In the meantime, such a young woman finds herself disappointed, disillusioned, and insecure, not knowing what direction to take. She may choose to prop up her husband, becoming more like a mother than a wife or friend. She may develop skills of domination, manipulation, or deceit. I have seen numerous situations in which a woman is shrill in her insistence that the man "is the head of the relationship, the leader" and that she is submissive to his leadership, while anyone who knows the pair sees otherwise. The negative patterns set in this kind of marriage or working relationship often plague the people in it for years and make it nearly impossible for them to learn to love, trust, encourage, and partner with each other.

Closely aligned with the disrespect and misunderstanding of head-ship and submission displayed by Christian women is a willingness to help in ways that are not actually helpful. I would suggest that such helpfulness is in truth harmful and that we should repent of it. Even if our desires are honorable, when we women are too "helpful," we interfere with men's abilities to take responsibility, to be accountable, and to grow.

Several years ago, I was sitting in the office of a female professor and colleague who had just facilitated a guided study that I was doing for my doctorate. The topic was on leadership and I said, "Angie, I know that I am a strong leader. I see it in my life, but I don't seem to inspire leadership in others." Without even taking a breath she said, "It's because you don't allow those around you to fail. You make sure, in fact, that they don't." I was stunned. As I sat there for a few minutes and reflected on her comment, I realized that she had named a weakness that was obvi-ous to others but not to me. She was absolutely right. I am often prone to be so helpful that I annoy others and interfere with their abilities to function fully. I have since repented of this sin. I have also realized that my tendency to be so helpful is not only harmful to others but gets in the way of God's work in various situations. Causing others to be depen-dent on me may make me feel important or allow me to be a hero, but it interferes in inappropriate ways with the far healthier relationships that others need to form with God.

Women should also repent of their propensity to turn our faces from the sin and weakness of our Christian brothers. Too often we are afraid to confront them in love, and we fail to call them to the high standard of Jesus' lordship and manhood. Although men need to meet in groups to pray for one another and hold each other accountable, they also need the input of sisters, wives, and friends. In fact, I am confident that men can sometimes hear a difficult message more clearly from a woman than from another man, whether because of different power dynamics, levels of intimacy, or communication patterns.

The romanticizing of male and female relationships is another area in which women must pay attention. Women readily cry "foul" in response to the prevalence of pornography and men's participation in the market. But while porn is marketed primarily to men, women are encouraged to embrace romantic novels, television programs, and movies. Often the female characters portrayed in these stories are weak-willed, easily overtaken, and especially vulnerable. Occasionally, they are also seductive, irresistible, and wildly passionate. The male characters, on the other hand, are endowed with incredible sexual prowess, great physical attributes, and the ability to discern what a woman truly wants even if she does not know it. Such media train women to take on inferior identities and to objectify men. I would ask all of us to consider more closely this area of seemingly harmless fun. Is it common for us to become so caught up in so-called romantic notions that we lose sight of what is really important in any relationship?

Think about how women often talk about the prom or other romantic social events. I have frequently heard these described as "your chance to be a real princess" or "the most romantic night of your life." With such an emphasis on the fleeting opportunity to experience love and glamour, how can we be surprised when so many young people decide to end their evenings in hotel rooms? I would suggest that even the way we often play up the magic of a wedding and how the bride looks—instead of the significance of the vows—can fall within the realm of this overemphasis on romance. Please don't think I don't love romance—Jack can testify that I do—but I believe that Christian women need to be very careful, maybe even repentant, about our participation in an inappropriate romantic focus. Flirtation and fantasy have their places, but they're not a foundation on which to build and sustain godly partnership with Christian men.

Women must also pay attention to how we often turn our hurt, frustration, and confusion about the difficulties in our relationships with men into excuses for anger, bitterness, wrath, sarcasm, and cynicism. Instead of being able to confront and let go of the hurts of the past, we too often cower and wrap ourselves in cloaks of woundedness that become our identity markers, and we lose ourselves in them. Carried over many years, these sinful and negative emotions warp our characters, damage our relationships, and leave little space for the Spirit to bear fruit in our lives. Women with these characteristics often find themselves alone because others can no longer bear the weight of their negativity. Their physical health may suffer as a result of the stress, and their emotional well-being is almost always altered. I imagine that as you have read these words, you have either pictured a woman who fits the description or seen yourself in them. Once again, let me be the first to confess.

I have had to work on anger issues most of my life. I have hurt my husband, offended my colleagues and students, challenged my friends, and scarred my children, but I never meant to do any of those things. Abused as a child, I learned at an early age to stand up for myself and to take care of myself no matter what. Through extensive counseling, faithful prayer, valued accountability, and loads of love, I am now a woman who is not angry anymore. I have been delivered by God's grace from that debilitating reality—it is not who I am. Scripture speaks volumes about the alternatives we are to have in Christ. When we are angry, we are to settle the matter quickly (Matt. 5:21–26). When vengeance is our motivation, we are to serve the other instead of seeking our rights (5:38–42). Although it is common to love a neighbor and hate an enemy, Jesus challenges us and models for us what it means to love our enemies, to pray for those who would harm us (5:43–48). Rather than allowing negative and harmful emotions to take root, women should repent of them and work to build good relationships based on the foundation of Christian love, patience, kindness, and service. But we must also be aware that these choices are not about a passive role but rather an active one. They are gifts of the Spirit that empower us to live fruitful and fulfilling lives. This deep surrender and desire for peace must not be used to keep women in subordinate positions or abusive relationships.

One final area in which I would call Christian women to repent is in our failure to be all that God has called us to be and to use the gifts and talents given to us by God. Too often we seem to fear that our strength or abilities will either intimidate or demean those around us. Yet this way of thinking is equally damaging to both females and males. To fear that our strength and capabilities will negatively affect others is demeaning to others and to ourselves. Even more significantly, such notions also demean God by indicating our failure to trust that God knew what was best in designing our unique strengths.

These challenges are not intended to give Christian women license to be insensitive, overbearing, or prideful in any sense, but then, in my experience with women, we are more prone to insecurity, hesitancy, and uncertainty. As we repent of holding back in being what God has created and empowered us to be, I would call us to practice true Christian humility. True humility, contrary to what many of us have thought, is not putting ourselves down or denying our God-given strengths. Rather it is standing tall, arms outstretched, embracing all that we are and can be before God.[4] In this position, I am also free to worship our great God, the one who made me and loves me. As a woman made in God's image,

I am free to live out a life of service and surrender that truly glorifies the Lord and blesses all partnerships in which I live and work.

Thoughts on Working Together

"First thing I learned is the importance of shutting up. I like to talk. I also think I am a relatively intelligent person whose ideas are often pertinent and insightful to the issue at hand. However, I am not the definitive source of valid answers, nor am I consistently right. Furthermore, even if I did have something valuable to contribute, was my contribution going to inadvertently discourage other group members, who probably have something equally valid and insightful to say, from speaking? Therefore, I attempted to listen first and speak second or even third. I learned that sometimes this meant not discussing something I thought to be important in exchange for creating space for others to express their ideas. Being quiet is hard work. However in the midst of my silence, true communal discernment and planning were able to take place. Often, I would hear an idea that never crossed my mind. Furthermore, my silence invited the more timid of the group to speak up. As time progressed, I would be asked for my opinion on a matter. This is significant because often in the past I would have been the first to give it."

—Male Student

A Call to Christian Men

In light of what I have just written, I must prayerfully shed the fear that is natural in addressing my Christian brothers and calling them to repentance. If godly partnership is to be achieved between men and women, there are areas to which men must give special attention as well. To begin with, I believe that Christian men must repent of the numerous ways in which they buy into a more secular rather than a sacred understanding of their masculinity. Our culture often portrays men as hapless, helpless creatures that cannot manage even the simplest task, much less function as responsible adults. This view is one that I hear referenced frequently in conversations with both men and women.

Men who accept this view of themselves often assume the role of a child in relation to women they see as potential mothers. In this position, the man becomes even more helpless, avoids confrontation with his angry "parent," and lives in an arrested state of maturity. Just as women should not over-function in a godly partnership, neither should men under-function.

To counteract this tendency, many Christians fall into the trap of prescribing roles for the woman and the man that are specific to each gender. He is to be strong, courageous, unafraid, unyielding—a warrior, a hunter, a mighty man. She is to be constant, nurturing, sensitive, submissive—a caregiver, a lover, a gentle woman. All of these qualities are godly ones, but are they unique to one gender or the other? Which of these attributes are most present in Jesus and, therefore, desirable in all of our lives? Which of these characteristics do we want for our sons and daughters? Surely to embody *all* of these traits and more, regardless of gender, is to live as we were created in God's image and to reflect the new life we have been given in Jesus Christ.

Closely related to the tendency to prescribe particular roles and their elements to each gender is a propensity for stereotyping. While none of us is ever completely free from tendencies to develop expectations and opinions of others, we must be careful how they are applied. Just as Christian women must not partake of misandry, neither should Christian men. When people universally apply expectations of what a "real" man is like, they contribute to the dismissal and demeaning of men who do not fit this limited mold, including those who display characteristics considered particularly feminine. It hurts all of us when Christian men make cruel and divisive comments about their brothers. Repenting for these attitudes is the only appropriate Christian response and the only one that enables the development of meaningful relationships.

Participation in misogyny, the demeaning or hatred of women, is equally unacceptable from Christian men. Although less socially acceptable than misandry in our current cultural climate, misogyny is equally damaging to the men who propagate it as to the women who are wounded by it. Telling sexist stories, crude jokes, or making derogatory comments that demean women may get a laugh from others, make a man appear cool in certain settings, and perhaps even bond him with other immature men, but at what cost? Such practices sully the Christian witness, damage the well-being of both men and women, and hamper the development of significant partnership. They also dishonor God in whose image both male and female are made.

I know that it would be easy to stop the discussion and the call to repentance here. I would be relieved and so would most men, perhaps even the women. But in our efforts to be true partners in the gospel, silence at this point would be inadvisable, even unfaithful. So where do I see sexism among my Christian brothers? Unfortunately, in many places, both subtle and easily apparent. Let me give some examples.

Imagine my surprise when a Sunday school teacher discussing creation from Genesis to the high school class introduced his lesson with a joke that everyone seemed to find hilarious. He said, "When God created the earth and all that was in it, he rested. After God created man, he rested. Then God created woman and since then neither God nor man has rested." Or I remember taking a graduate class and after making comments about the text we were studying, a fellow student asked if I was Jack's wife. When I said yes, he dismissed me by saying, "No wonder you know so much about Scripture." (Jack is the dean of our university's

College of Biblical Studies.) Or I think of a gathering of Christian professionals I attended at which the chairman of the organization told a joke
about a man physically abusing his wife. Everyone laughed, and I doubt
that anyone took the time to talk to him about the inappropriateness of
his humor. I know I didn't.

Incidents can be as overt as these or as subtle as calling women
"ladies" or "girls," or refusing to acknowledge women who serve on the
foreign field as missionaries, not just the wives of missionaries, or making
comments that imply all women love to shop or can't drive. I have heard
such statements made too often from pulpits and Bible classes with
apparently no awareness of their offensiveness. But perhaps especially
challenging is the prevalent, often exclusive, use of masculine pronouns
and images to speak of God without ever considering the feminine meta-
phors for God found in Scripture, and the failure to use gender-inclusive
language in songs, sermons, and prayers so that the whole congregation
feels welcomed and valued. These forms of sexism often go unnoticed
and unchallenged in many of our churches.

Churches in which masculine language and images are used ex-
clusively also contribute to a sense of male entitlement that is simply
unacceptable among Christian brothers and sisters. It is another area
for repentance. Although we live in a pluralistic society that generally
shuns paternalism, patriarchy, and hierarchy, these elements remain
deeply rooted in some of our Christian communities, especially in certain regions.

Several years ago, a group of women asked me to develop an equipping program for elders' wives. (It took me a while to find others willing
to address the real ministry of such women. This example itself is evidence
of entitlement when we assume that only men are fulfilling the work of
certain roles.) The first two sessions were just for women, and everyone
attending participated freely. The last session was a panel discussion for
both husbands and wives, and I was absolutely stunned by what transpired.

The discussion was lively and engaging for the men. They spoke to the women on the panel, asking questions and making comments, but *not one* of the women in the audience said a word.

In a final evaluative meeting where we discussed the day and what should come next, I turned the tape recording off so that everyone was free to participate. I asked the women for candid feedback and questioned why they let the discussion go as it did. Shame-faced and frustrated, they said that they rarely if ever spoke up when their husbands were present. One woman, with tears running down her face, said that when they were younger she and her husband discussed everything, but once he took a leadership role at church, they no longer talked about most church-related issues. She shared further how these developments hindered their sense of partnership and even their ability to pray together. If these hindrances exist in the strong, godly marriages we seek to be leaders in the church, what must they be like for our young married couples and for single women and men? What possibility is there for godly partnerships to flourish in such environments?

I would suggest that too many of us have been formed by the presupposition, whether or not we state it, that to be male is to be superior. Although few would openly acknowledge that the converse is true—that to be female is to be inferior—if we believe the first presupposition at any level then the second must also be true. Obviously there are churches and relationships in which women and men function as equals, but there are not enough. To be male, then, in situations like the one described is to be privileged, whether that privilege is obvious or not. To uncover some hidden expectations, we might consider a few questions: Who sits in the preferred seats at church? How are our cry rooms set up—for women only or for all parents with small children? Who works in the nursery and teaches small children? When strong opinions are expressed, whose are most likely to be valued? What are the leadership roles at church, and are they open to both men and women?

Another area where men, like women, must repent is in misunderstandings of headship and submission. The assumptions that many Christian men make in this regard are actually antithetical to biblical teaching. One such assumption is that all men hold positions of authority over all women. The context of Ephesians 5, from which we take much of our understanding of headship and submission, however, is clearly that of the family. The reference, still touchy, is to the husband being the head of his wife as Christ is the head of the church, not to all men in general being heads over all women. Regardless, we in the church too readily perpetuate the sense of any man being the natural leader in any situation.

Jack and I frequently encounter young couples in counseling who, when quizzed about their understanding of these delicate matters, will say that they think the man being head of the home means that he makes the final decision, has the final word. Jack's comment at that point is usually, "So the man always gets his way?" "No!" they respond, "but somebody has to make a decision." Their response then is generally more practical than biblical, more about who is in charge and how authority works. Christ's headship of the church is not exhibited by the making of decisions about the well-being of the bride. Rather, Christ perfectly models headship by giving up self and dying for us, making the church pure and blameless in the process. In many ways, the reference to Christ's sacrifice means that as the head, Jesus assumes an even more surrendered position than the church. In truth, submission is mutual and life-giving for Christ and the church, as well as for husbands and wives, and for all believers. This understanding of male headship not only disallows male dominance, which is as damaging to men as it is to women, but it also promotes the development of healthy partnerships of all kinds.

Closely aligned with the subject of headship and submission is an expectation we should all have that Christian men will partner in providing comfort, shelter, and protection for society's weakest members. While this value may be found in secular culture, it is central to what

God has demanded of covenant people. From the giving of the Law in the Hebrew Bible through Jesus' own teaching, Scripture is full of challenges for people of faith to take care of the poorest of the poor. And often it is women and children who are most in need of assistance and have few resources. I would call Christian men to these front lines and have them share the burden of meeting the needs of those who are in the greatest need of protection.

Several years ago, I spoke at a women's conference. During one of the small group sessions, a woman quietly asked to speak to me and confided some serious marital problems. We prayed together, and I encouraged her to seek help from her local church. About two weeks later, I received a phone call from her, and as the story unfolded it was apparent that her husband had been physically abusing her for some time. He had just beaten her up and even threatened their small child before driving off in a rage. I encouraged her to report all of these facts to the local police, but she didn't feel it would do any good—she had been down that road before. I then asked if anyone at church knew. She told me that about six months before she had confided in one of the men at church who served as an elder. He said he would talk with her husband and then encouraged her to work even harder at being a good wife, so that there would be no reason to criticize her.

I advised this woman to take their child and go to that elder's home immediately. She told me the elders, all men, were meeting at the church as we spoke. I then suggested that she go to the whole group and tell them what she had told me. She was hesitant, but I asked her to address these men with courage and conviction. "Ask them," I said, "what they would want the men of the church to do if you were their daughter, granddaughter, or sister?" This woman followed my advice, and I am so pleased at the response of this group of godly men. They immediately made all the provisions needed for this mother and child. They engaged the local police in getting a restraining order against the abusive husband.

A couple of them set up an accountability structure for him, and they enrolled the young family in therapy. When I heard from this Christian sister, almost a year later, things were still challenging, but she and her family were making progress. These godly men not only provided appropriate comfort and protection for this woman and her child, they also partnered with her and her husband in ways that were effective and meaningful.

Two other understandings of men prevalent in the world and too frequently accepted as true, even among Christians, are that the male ego and male libido are forces that are "out of their control." We must discard these ideas as faulty and un-Christian. As a young woman, I remember frequently being warned by older women not to wound a man's pride. While I understand that care and consideration should be given to the feelings of others, I have often wondered why we consider men so weak and immature that they cannot handle challenging situations and relationships without having their egos damaged. A reading of Proverbs clearly indicates that pride has no place in a humble life of faith. Just as Christian women should not put themselves down and remain unconfident and insecure, so also godly men should purge themselves of a propensity toward pride and a fragility in dealing with it.

In raising our son, Jack and I frequently reminded him that we do not buy into the perspectives that "boys will be boys," that he needed "to sow his wild oats," or that there was anything in his life that he could not, with God's help, control. Granted, I do not know what it is like to be male, but I know that Jesus Christ came in the form of a man, and he managed not only to live a life that was pure and sinless, but he also called others to the same standard. Do we dare ask less of our Christian men and boys? Yes, sexual urges are strong, but when placed under the lordship of Christ and held in accountability by the community of faith, they are not uncontrollable. I applaud the efforts by many churches to form men's groups to call Christian brothers to repent of sexual sin and reclaim godly lives. I pray that we as Christian sisters may make the journey with them in faithful partnership.

Men must also acknowledge and repent of their hesitancy to confront believing women who struggle with sins of all kinds. Just as women need to journey with their faltering Christian brothers, so the men must reciprocate and hold women to the standard of image-bearers of God and new creations in Christ. Failure to be able "to speak the truth in love" means that all of us are hindered in becoming the mature and holy community desired by God. In such instances, we are held hostage by our lowest impulses instead of raised by our highest ones. Just as men can often hear a message most clearly from a woman, so I think a woman sometimes can best hear what is needed from a man, who can speak helpfully from an outside perspective. Yet we rarely engage one another at these levels of confrontation, communication, and confession.

The final areas where repentance may be needed have to do with strength, control, and dominance. I would first challenge Christian men to abandon any negativity about dealing with strong women. Strength in and of itself is a quality to be desired by both genders as it is surrendered to and fueled by a relationship with the Lord. Yet a woman in the church who is strong must frequently use care not to appear "too strong." I have watched numerous situations in which a woman expressed her opinion with passion and conviction or her anger at some injustice and the men all either backed off, clammed up, or ignored her concerns completely. A common suspicion seems to be that a strong woman naturally wants to control. If she does, of course, these negative tendencies should certainly be addressed forthrightly, but why would we automatically associate confidence and boldness with a desire to dominate?

Many reasons may exist for men to avoid relating with strong women—including the sense that such confrontation may be more harmful than helpful to all involved, a hesitation to engage in a verbal contest with little hope of resolution, or anxiety about possible miscommunication because of social gender expectations—but these feelings need not become barriers that hinder men from reaching out to women who need godly male perspectives and presences in their lives as part of their belonging to the community of faith.

Recently in one of my classes at ACU, a male student said, "I would rather tangle with your husband any day than with you." Many in the room laughed. I was curious, so I asked him to explain. He said he felt intimidated by my intensity; he had a preconceived idea of what I must be like even though we've had little contact with each other, and he was afraid that a confrontation would somehow demean his masculine identity. I was grateful for the classroom conversation. It cleared up some obvious tensions that I could sense between myself and my male students, and it also opened new doors of discovery for all of us about ourselves and our relationship.

In the world, and unfortunately sometimes in the church, men have historically wielded the most power. Strength for men is a virtue; cultivating that strength leads to high power and position. Dominance and control have sometimes been viewed not only as male gender norms but even as attributes to be valued. Exercising these qualities is the way to get ahead. But I am confident that any one of us could tell a number of stories of leaders who misused their power and abused individuals in their care with devastating results for all concerned. Power is intrinsically neither good nor bad, and neither gender is automatically better at holding power. Both women and men must choose to use power responsibly, for the benefit of all.

Christian men have nothing to fear in embracing the God-empowered, gifted, and called leadership of women. Accepting that a faithful woman can be used by God for good purposes should do nothing to undermine male leadership. It is time for us to move beyond acknowledgment of the problems in this area and find solutions to address them. It is time for Christian men who believe these truths to speak out and to act upon them. It is time for us to join together in godly partnership. The home, the church, and the world are in need of our working together in the Kingdom as we join God in all that God is doing in the world.

Thoughts on Working Together

"I am constantly growing in appreciation of the differences that lie within the genders, and yet still all too often [I am] simply frustrated. . . . I know that [I will have] a lifetime of growing in relationship with men. In the end, all too often I come to the conclusion that men and women will not really ever understand each other. Despite the constant differences, it is times with the opposite sex that can grow me the most—perhaps because [men bring a perspective] that I do not see myself. I really enjoyed spending time within our group, despite any conflict or tension. It was refreshing to be around people who are different than me and to learn and grow with and from them. My teammates have so many good things to offer and I was amazed at how much we grew in our knowledge and love for each other. I really did see how our growth with each other . . . was the direct effect of time together. Another life principle here I suppose! You will grow in the area that you put your time. You can't get more basic than that!"

—Female Student

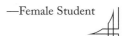

Conclusion

At the New Wineskins retreat, I was unprepared for the response from those listening to my presentation. Preaching is not something that I am terribly familiar with, since in most congregations of my denominational affiliation, women don't preach. Add to that my lack of experience with large gatherings of predominantly African American preachers, and you can imagine how it felt when everyone stood about halfway through my presentation. But they didn't just stand there.

The moment I began to call men and women to repentance and to reclaim what God intended for our partnerships, the place erupted. Folks were clapping their hands and shouting out responses.

What I thought might disrupt my train of thought in presenting the material rather served to fuel the message. I found myself speaking with a passion and intensity that surprised even me. Obviously I had hit a nerve. No, God used me to hit a nerve. Something fundamentally necessary was spoken that day.

I have been changed by my partnership with my colleagues, both male and female, as we have journeyed together over many years. But this one single event and the message God spoke through me that day also seriously altered how I think about partnership and how I try to live it out daily. I hope this chapter has done the same for its readers. Careful examination and repentance is challenging, but once we begin to reclaim God's intentions for how we ought to live together, we can start building godly partnerships that are successful and satisfying.

Notes to Chapter Two

1. Ruth Haley Barton, *Equal to the Task: Men and Women in Partnership* (Downers Grove: InterVarsity, 1998), 15, emphasis hers.

2. A half century ago, Dorothy Sayers suggested that men and women be referred to as "neighboring" rather than opposite sexes [cf. "The Human-Not-Quite so Human," reprinted in Sayers, *Are Women Human?* (Downers Grove: InterVarsity Press, 1971), 37–47]. Quoted by Mary Stewart Van Leeuwen in "Opposite Sexes or Neighboring Sexes? What do the Social Sciences Really Tell Us?" in *Women, Ministry and the Gospel: Exploring New Paradigms,* eds. Mark Husbands and Timothy Larsen (Downers Grove: InterVarsity Press, 2007), 181.

3. Sarah Sumner, *Men and Women in the Church* (Downers Grove: InterVarsity, 2003), 298.

4. Gladys Hunt, *Ms. Means Myself: Being a Woman in an Uneasy World* (Grand Rapids: Zondervan, 1972), 17.

Chapter Three

Being Together
How We Can Grow in Partnership

My husband Jack and I were among the last of the small group to gather. We were excited to be with other young couples for an evening instead of just teenagers. Since Jack served the church as a youth minister and I taught at one of the local high schools, social time with peers was rare.

As we entered the house, we noticed that all the men were talking in the living room while the women were obviously working in the kitchen to finish the last details of the meal we would share together. Jack winked at me, took the dish I had been carrying, and walked into the kitchen.

He was greeted warmly and was soon very engaged in the conversation that centered mostly on children (diapers, toilet training, and bedtime difficulties), job struggles, and housework. The women were surprised at his level of expertise on their favorite topics and readily included him in the discussion.

I tentatively entered the living room where the men were involved in a rather intense discussion about politics and religion (how a Christian should respond to capital punishment, abortion, and organ donation). For the first few minutes I just listened to the lively conversation but soon I jumped right into the conversation.

It was definitely the most interesting discussion I had with anyone that week, and the men seemed surprised that I had such strong opinions on these topics. I'm not sure, however, that my involvement was well received. As the evening progressed, I had a nagging sense that some of those gathered felt that I might have stepped out of my place.

Jack thought the evening went great and was determined to continue this practice whenever possible just to "mix things up" a little. (Anyone who knows Jack would not be surprised at this revelation.) The encounter left me wondering why we are at times so comfortable and at ease with each other as men and women while on other occasions we seem insecure and uncertain.

———————— ⚓ ————————

Experiences like these vary as widely as the people involved in them. They occur at home, on the job, and in the church. The question of why some mixed gender relationships function with ease and effectiveness while others do not is something I have thought about extensively. Several years ago, when challenged to plan and implement an intervention in the context of my ministry as part of the Doctor of Ministry program, I saw a unique opportunity for deeper investigation of this question. At that time, our department (Bible, Missions, and Ministry) didn't give attention to how male and female majors could be better equipped to work together. Since I team-taught a two-course sequence of the students' required classes with two male colleagues, my dissertation committee and I decided that I would construct my project to address this significant issue and implement my work in these courses.

My first step was to place the students in the first course into intentionally mixed-gender learning teams. Over the course of the project, the ratio between men and women varied from 3:1 to 6:1, depending on course enrollment. In the first semester, my colleagues and I gave various team assignments that encouraged them to get to know one another and to learn to work effectively together. In the second semester, we kept the same groups basically intact and assigned them a service-learning project that they worked on throughout the course. At the end of that term, we conducted focus groups to see how well students developed godly partnership within their teams. Although the data collected indicated mixed results—some respondents indicated growth, while others felt they gained nothing—six key principles emerged from their collective insights.

Thoughts on Working Together

"I must admit that upon first glance I felt there was no difference between the roles [our female team member] played compared to us guys. However upon further consideration and reflection, I began to notice one major difference. [She] did all the work; we simply did what she said. To me it was very much like the relationship I have with my mother: Her telling me what to do, to take care of this or that, and me simply doing them. Is this a struggle that is often mentioned? Is this one of the reasons that women are still struggling so much in their roles? Mothers, at least my mother, are overworked and underappreciated. Is the same problem in the church? I suspect it is. I also felt if truth were told we picked [on our female teammate] more than each other, it was out of fun and simply joking around, but [she] did seem to get the brunt of a lot of those times."

—Male Student

1. Sharing Their Stories

Telling stories is important to the formation of individuals, families, cultures, and religion. By telling our stories, we discover who we are and we pass on our heritage, with all of its embedded values and tradition. Through story we come to better understand not only ourselves but also others, to make connections, and to share our goals and dreams. It is not surprising then that in our study, groups who shared their stories with one another reported greater effectiveness in their work and greater enjoyment of the overall process.

The Hebrew Bible and the Christian New Testament tell a continuous story of God's involvement with the created world and the unfolding, ongoing redemption of God's people. Yet the story is also one of the people's sins, failure, discouragement, bondage, and betrayal. Without these stories, we would know little about God or how we were called and formed into being God's people. Even when God gives the Law to Israel, the commandments are couched in story. As Moses delivers the Ten Commandments to the people in the wilderness, they begin with a story: "I am the Lord your God, who brought you out of the land of Egypt, out of the house of slavery; you shall have no other gods before me" (Exod. 20:2–3). God speaks volumes to Israel in this simple statement of what was done on their behalf. They cannot forget; it is their story. It is important for us to see our lives of faith as a continuation of the biblical story. Faith lives on; it grows stronger as we tell it and deeper as we examine it. Sin still exists, and when we share our struggles, we can receive comfort, accountability, and forgiveness. God is still alive and active in the world guiding, teaching, and delivering; we need to tell one another exactly how. Yet few of us see our lives either as a story or as a contribution to the larger narrative.

Several years ago, I was at a conference with two colleagues with whom I taught in the public schools. As we spent several days together telling stories, sharing wisecracks, and enjoying each other's company, one woman said to me, "Everything exciting seems to happen to you. Nothing ever happens to me." I laughed and said that her statement couldn't be true because some of my best stories came out of our shared experiences as colleagues; I'm just always looking for the story. I assume that even the smallest happenings somehow will make the story more interesting and help me learn more about myself and others. My students and friends can testify to how much I love to hear and to tell a good story. When my two male colleagues from the team-taught courses and I presented at a conference a few years ago, we found our teaching relationships greatly enhanced by the experience. We had time to share our stories, to really get to know one another better. We achieved even greater partnership.

Much of my love of stories comes from my family, from growing up in a small town, and from a vivid imagination. Telling stories in the past was the way people passed their time and formed their collective memory. Today other forms of entertainment have replaced storytelling on the front porch or in the living room, and we often claim to be too busy to spend a whole evening sharing deeply with one another. Yet I do not know of a time when people long more for a sense of belonging, of community, to truly know other people and to be known by them. We need to share our stories. Failure to do so often leads to false intimacy, shallow relationships, and immature partnership. Telling our stories is central to the development of godly partnership.

Among our student teams, two types of group consistently developed effective partnership. The first was those whose members already knew one another before they were assigned to their learning teams and who shared a sense of respect for one another and a commitment to working well together. The second was those whose members made knowing and understanding one another a high priority in completing their shared assignment. Both types of group took time to share their stories and to pray for each other. They recognized that stories couldn't be told only once but are ongoing, dynamic entities that happen to us on a daily basis and that change as we learn to interpret them over time. Our stories must be shared again and again so that we can learn more and more about each other even when we think we already know.

One day when I was speaking in chapel at ACU, I referenced the life-changing experience I had in college with the death of my first husband, Mike. Jack, to whom I had been married for over twenty years at that time, came up to me after the presentation. He said that there was one little detail I had shared that day that really helped him to understand the whole experience better. Neither one of us remembers today what that detail was; it has now become part of the larger fabric of that story (and we are getting too old to remember such specific things). The important thing is that Jack had heard me tell Mike's story since the first day we met, but that day in chapel, we grew in relationship and understanding because of a small detail I'd finally remembered to share.

Telling our stories also allows equal footing for all involved. Differences in gender, ethnicity, age, and social status often diminish as we come to know and understand our common humanity better. We can better handle irritating traits or habits when we understand their origins, and hearing the context in which certain perspectives formed can enrich our lives as we strive to be God's people in an increasingly complex environment. Sharing who we are allows us to make connections that we might otherwise miss and to support one another more effectively. Telling our stories inevitably offers the opportunity for us to connect to the larger story of God's work in the world. All of these elements of sharing story inform the development of partnership, making it more meaningful and potentially more effective.

2. Finding Their Center

Organized groups tend to meet for reasons they know, whether their goal is simple socialization and the formation of friendships or accomplishing a specific task or project. Yet I would suggest that in a Christian context, groups also have a higher purpose: finding the center of who we are and what we do in the Lord.

In a testy encounter, a young lawyer asks Jesus what he must do to inherit eternal life. Jesus turns the question back to the man by asking how he reads the Law. The man responds, "You shall love the Lord your God with all your heart, and with all your soul, and with all your strength, and with all your mind; and your neighbor as yourself." And Jesus said to him, "You have given the right answer; do this, and you will live" (Luke 10:27–28). Similar encounters of testing or discussion can be found in both Matthew (22:34–40) and Mark (12:28–34). All three Gospels feature the same two passages from the Hebrew Bible: The first is known as the *shema* and is so central to Israel's understanding of who they are and how they are to live that Moses instructs the people to recite it to their children, talk about it at home and when they are away, when they lie down and when they rise, and to fix it on their persons and write it on their doorposts (Deut. 6:4–9). The second, about loving your neighbor, is found in Leviticus 19:18. And in Matthew, Jesus declares, "On these two commandments hang all the law and the prophets." Living with these at the forefront of our consciousness means that we are living out the sum of what God requires from us. But often we are tempted, as the young lawyer was, to justify ourselves in Jesus' presence. After hearing Jesus' reply, the lawyer asks another famous question, "And who is my neighbor?" Jesus responds by telling the familiar story of the Good Samaritan. Here we learn that we bear responsibility to love the most unlikely people, those who may be outsiders or even enemies—and we bear this responsibility because of our relationship with God.

So what does all this have to do with mixed gender groups and finding a center when working in them? It means that we see every situation, relationship, and assignment as an opportunity to grow in love both with God and with our neighbor. Our purpose is not merely to form social connections or complete a task but to live out these injunctions in all that we do.

Gender constitutes one of the most prevalent forms of diversity—the vast majority of us interact with more than one gender every day. As we live and work with one another, we are offered the opportunity to grow to love people quite different from ourselves and yet people who share our basic humanity. Too often, we fall prey to the temptation to assume that all men are one way and all women another. We may choose to stereotype each other instead of learning about our wide and wonderful variety, as well as our enriching similarity; we dismiss one another, thinking that the tasks before us are too time-consuming to waste time on "touchy-feely" experiences; or we may joke about our differences and assume that we can't really understand one another. Yet none of these responses reflects the challenge of living out the two great commandments. Loving God means loving all that comes from God, and bearing God's image means that we each carry something of God's essence within us.

Several years ago, Jack and I banned the words "You just don't understand" from our family's conversations. We were in the middle of raising teenagers and the words were too easily spoken; they automatically distanced us from one another causing greater barriers and deeper hurt. We assured our children that one of our greatest desires was to understand and support them, and when we misunderstood each other, it was time for us to sit down, pray, talk, listen, and come to a place where we could lovingly be together instead of discounting one another. It was our way of being neighbors to each other.

Through my years of working with student learning teams, I have seen clearly that students' maturity levels are as varied as their personalities, cultures, and experiences. Some of them entered the project by closing themselves off from any form of learning and consequently consistently reported little or no growth through the whole process. Others came with wonderful attitudes, ready to embrace not only the learning experience but also their colleagues in the project. Still others had less openness to the whole process but grew to see that they could learn a great deal if they let themselves.

These responses are no different than what we all encounter on a regular basis in the varied situations in which we are called to work with each other as men and women. If our goal is simply to socialize or to complete a task, chances are good that we will meet it. If, however, we see the overarching purpose of working with those who are different from us as an opportunity to grow more in love with God and each other, we will have found our true center. It is never an easy pursuit, but it is always a worthwhile one.

3. Learning to Communicate

Volumes have been written on the need for and ways to better communication. It is an area of broad research and deep need for all of us, and I will admit that I enter this phase of the writing with a little bit of trepidation. Yet throughout my study, every learning team and each focus group discussed the need for good communication between women and men. It was the factor that all agreed needed the most concentration and work.

At the most foundational level, just keeping each other informed is important. But going beyond basic communication requires that we continually give something up, that we try to see things from another's perspective, that we value and honor the contributions of all, and that we learn to encourage, support, and hold one another accountable. Recognizing that communicating is never an easy task makes the discussion of it at least a little less intimidating.

One of the most important initial tasks in working in any diverse group is identifying and assessing the overall make-up of the individuals involved. Is there a dominant culture, race, social class, age, or gender? Who is likely to be advantaged or disadvantaged in the team effort and why? What are the various personalities at play in the situation? How can we best work together to ensure that everyone involved feels both empowered and safe? The first two areas of discussion—telling our stories and finding our center—are excellent starting points and lead to the most natural and important form of communication among Christians: prayer.

Praying for and with one another brings the whole group to God in a surrendered posture of equality, humility, and need. Prayer unites us when we are divided, instructs us about areas in which we need to grow, quiets us when we need to listen, and reminds us of what is really significant about our work and relationships. Prayer also helps us to develop trust in God and one another.

Closely tied with praying together is the formation of a spiritual covenant. Some would call it setting ground rules or defining parameters for the group, but for Christians working together, I think the task has a much more spiritual dimension. It is what helps us not only find but also *keep* our center. A spiritual covenant is a document that the group formulates and commits to respect. It outlines such things as how we will talk and listen to one another, how we will divide work and meet deadlines, in what ways we will hold one another accountable, and how we commit to spiritual discipline during the tenure of our work together.

No specific rules exist for setting these guidelines; any given group can negotiate terms that will meet their particular needs. Through forming a spiritual covenant, we remind each other that the individuals involved and the relationships formed are of greater importance than the projects completed. It also governs our communication and interaction in a way that honors and supports everyone involved.

The process of setting the spiritual covenant is an excellent time for self-examination on the part of team members. All of us carry prejudices and stereotypes that we must address if we are to journey together in partnership and learn to love God and one another more. Some of these prejudices and stereotypes are subtle and ill-defined, while others are quite clear.

A few years ago, I was asked to chair one of the university-wide accreditation committees. Various members were selected from across the spectrum of administration, faculty, and staff. We were scheduled to meet for an hour each week to accomplish the process of evaluating one area of the university for accreditation. During the first meeting, we spent time getting acquainted, setting our covenant, and determining how we would begin the work before us. I told everyone I would send an email outlining the tasks more specifically. Each person was to select an area in which they would focus their contributions to our overall task by the next committee meeting.

As we were leaving, a well-respected administrator came up to me and said in a rather surprised tone, "That was a well-conducted meeting." I thanked him and started to walk away but decided that it would be better for the relationship for me to pause for a moment. He went on to tell me that he had dreaded being assigned to a committee led by a woman because everyone knew that we tend to be more focused on emotion and relationship than on getting the job done. As our conversation continued, he admitted that this assumption on his part had made it difficult for him to work with women in the past. We sat there for a while, laughing and sharing other situations in which our responses had been less than desirable. The ability to share these, to ask for forgiveness, and to not take offense meant that we found common ground that day from which we could work together and relate more effectively.

This incident points to another critical issue in good communication—the willingness to share openly. It would have been easy for my male colleague to keep his stereotype to himself. He could have continued to be something of a critic, or he could have shared his opinion inappropriately with others on the committee, creating divisions and further prejudices.

All of us have been guilty of all of these inappropriate responses at one time or another. But his decision to share his bias with the one who had the potential to be most affected by it in the situation showed both courage and strength. He shared with me not knowing what my response would be, but he took a risk that benefitted us both. I admire and appreciate my colleague for his openness.

Closely related to the willingness to be open is the importance of listening to one another. It is perhaps the most difficult dimension of our interpersonal relationships. Listening takes time, patience, and skill, and many of us are already pressed with tight schedules, demanding workloads, and family responsibilities. So how do we learn to listen attentively and carefully? One key is to focus only on what the other is saying, without planning what we want to say as soon as there's a pause in the conversation. Listening to all that others have to say before responding is a wonderful spiritual practice that frees us to know others more completely. For those of us who are prone to be more talkative than others, listening intently frees us from the need to say something significant ourselves and gives voice to those who speak less frequently. In those moments, we learn to value the rich insights of our quieter friends and colleagues. I have grown to appreciate what I call "practicing the presence of God."

I first learned this approach when visiting other countries where I did not understand the language but wanted to know what people were saying. In these contexts, I ask the Lord to be with me, giving me eyes to see and ears to hear—gifts that can only come from God. What happens in these moments is that I grow more attuned to the speakers' mannerisms, their body language, and the contexts from which they are speaking. In these moments, I am able to hear in whole new ways and to see what I might otherwise have missed. Through these experiences, I grow in my ability to be still and alert, to be aware and engaged even when it is challenging, and to see and hear the whole person not just the words they are saying—all skills needed for greater listening.

4. Knowing When to Step Up or Step Down

In my research study, one of the recurring elements of discussion among students was about leadership within their learning teams. Because all of these men and women were enrolled as majors in the Department of Bible, Missions, and Ministry, they were usually recognized as good leaders among their peers. Putting people like this together and then seeing who assumed leadership was interesting. The majority of the teams followed one of five general patterns.

Some groups went with what I call a *default method* of leadership selection. They allowed the most outspoken, opinionated, take-charge person to assume the primary leadership role. In these instances, the rest of the team usually rallied around the leader and got the work done efficiently and without too much difficulty. But when asked to measure how they achieved partnership, they usually reported minimal growth and learning.

Other groups involved in the project used a more *democratic approach*. In telling their stories, different leadership skills surfaced and as the students planned their project, they took a vote to see who might lead the group. Since democracy is the political system with which our students were most familiar, it tended to work well—everyone reported feeling involved in the decisions and free to express their opinions or to assume other leadership roles as they arose. In giving feedback, these teams usually reported achieving effective partnership and seemed generally satisfied with the work they had done.

Still other groups struggled to decide who would lead them. This approach I call the *no-leadership* model. These groups usually faltered in making most decisions, and they often failed to complete the assignment professionally, or at all. Sometimes they were involved in power plays with two or more strong leaders vying for the primary role. At other times, no one wanted to assume leadership because things were not going well and none of the members wanted to "take the fall." Ironically, when reporting their perceived effectiveness, these groups often rated themselves highly, reinforcing the professors' assessment that they were unaware of what was really going on within their team.

Since gender is the greatest diversity the learning teams experience, I was interested to see that some of the groups practiced a *maternal leadership* model. In these situations, one female assumed responsibility for managing the schedules, communicating with everyone, and ensuring that deadlines were met and the project presented effectively. Some of these women used emotional tactics such as anger, tears, or martyr tendencies to cajole their teammates into getting the work done. Both the women who led and the team members who followed in these groups expressed frustration, and the ratings for the partnership achieved usually fell within the mid-range—not too high or too low.

The most effective leadership exhibited in the learning teams was among those who chose to share leadership in a more *collaborative approach*. These groups sought to recognize and use the many varied and rich gifts that each member brought to the task. In their reporting about partnership, these groups' members expressed not only a higher degree of satisfaction with their work but also a deeper appreciation for their team members and the partnership they achieved. Their attitude and motivation tended to remain fairly constant, and they seemed to learn the most about the project.

Since observing these group dynamics, I have noticed these same tendencies in the church. Often, we do not know how to select a leader within any given group and are tempted to use either the default or democratic methods of selection. Yet we rarely find satisfaction with these approaches. In other situations, we opt for the no-leadership or maternal approaches (or variations of these themes), but these usually lead to dissatisfaction. The collaborative model, so successful with the students, is uncommon in most communities of faith. By telling our stories, establishing a covenant, and learning to communicate, we make way for choosing leaders who will work collaboratively with others.

Perhaps one of the most significant indicators of potentially collaborative leaders is their ability to know when to step up and when to step down. Stepping up does not mean seizing leadership, but it does mean being brave enough to take charge when leadership is needed. It means being able to delegate tasks to others, encourage them as they complete their work, and follow through to make sure they have what they need to do the job. Stepping up means making sure that everyone in the group is heard, that all ideas are examined, and all contributions valued.

Stepping down as a collaborative leader means being willing to share leadership and not being threatened by the strengths and talents of others. A person willing to step down is not afraid to wait on process and recognizes that a prayerful position is perhaps the most powerful one. Collaborative leaders who step down know how to receive criticism and grow from it. They have control over their emotions and are good in conflict situations. This kind of leader is always looking for other potential leaders to mentor.

Although some individuals have more collaborative tendencies than others, anyone can develop the skills necessary to grow in this type of leadership. Godly partnerships are the best context, in my opinion, for us to learn how to better lead and serve one another. Working together we share our lives, find a common purpose, learn to communicate with one another, and develop leadership qualities that bless others. The church has a responsibility to encourage this form of development in both men and women and to put it to good use for the whole community.

5. Taking Responsibility for Self

All of these elements of building godly partnership require each individual to take responsibility for self in the context of relationship with God and others. Since an appropriate, God-given love of self is essential to loving our neighbors, we must give attention to each individual in our groups.

In many ways, the effectiveness of any team is equal only to the willingness of all members to own their parts of the group dynamic. In situations where the people involved are emotionally healthy and self-differentiated, teammates practice give-and-take while simultaneously focusing on the task before them. However, in groups with individuals who have not learned to take responsibility for self, set good boundaries, or model good self care, the group inevitably spends more time focused on these few people and less on the group as a whole or on anything they hoped to achieve.

Over eight years of research, I saw several patterns emerge that indicate difficulty in taking responsibility for self. Generally, individuals struggling in these areas seem to fall into two main categories—those who under-function and those who over-function. It is common for any team to have at least one or more members who have these tendencies. All of the steps suggested earlier—storytelling, spiritual covenanting, and good communication—are excellent tools to offset potential negative interactions in any group. When groups catch potential problems early and address them, members can prevent trouble by helping each other to abandon destructive tendencies through recognition and faithful accountability to others.

Before I go any further, however, I want to be clear. Conflict is not something to be avoided but rather is a natural, healthy, and inevitable part of interaction among any group of diverse people. Embracing conflict and working through it effectively is one measure of how well a group has formed relationship and trusts one another. Learning to stand together and identify issues, rather than blaming or shaming individuals, is a wonderful approach to conflict. Although I cannot cite here all patterns of under-functioning or over-functioning individuals, I chose a few examples that represent the most common difficulties my students encountered.

In those who under-function, several variations of the same theme can be identified by the cry, "It's not *my* fault." These individuals use any excuse possible for their failure to fully participate in the group. Generally they blame others—bosses, colleagues, friends, spouses, parents, and children, whoever is readily available—for their own lack of involvement or disruptive behaviors. Or they represent their lives as the busiest and most stressed, and therefore too important to be bothered with the needs of this group and its participants. One of my least favorite, and unfortunately most successful, tactics of under-functioning people is to discredit others (often the leadership) or the task itself. This mutinous tendency often begins small with a seemingly innocent question or a well-placed barb that can grow rapidly into out-and-out viciousness. Soon others join in and the result is troubling: gossip, slander, hurt feelings, or even derailment of the group or project.

For those that tend to over-function, a common statement might be "I'll *take care* of it." These individuals, unlike their under-functioning counterparts, tend to take on too much responsibility. They sign up for too many duties or take over what others have committed to do. The over-functioning team member is quick to correct people and tends to check up on them. This individual often supplies refreshments for every meeting or volunteers to take notes for everyone. What may at first appear as genuine Christian service soon takes on negative connotations. If the over-functioning team member joins forces with the under-functioning one, they create an incredibly codependent relationship that has the potential to challenge all group dynamics. The over-functioner enables the under-functioner to continue in negative behaviors and in turn is empowered to continue in his or her own negative behavior. The over-functioning team members will soon discover that their groups are willing to let them do it all. Instead of learning to collaborate, such a team surrenders to this needy person, and again, the results are disastrous.

Thoughts on Working Together

"[I] learned that it is okay for me to step us as a leader. I think that because I was the only girl in the group and it was somewhat expected of me to step up and be a leader that I shied away from it. Or perhaps I wasn't as much of a leader because I was the only one in the group and I didn't want people to think that meant I had to be the leader and I was gung-ho on woman power or something. However, there were several times where I knew at least one other person had something brewing in their mind and just needed someone to prompt them to start talking. It was necessary for me to step up and ask what they were thinking. I think . . . that it is fine for me to be a leader as long as I am humble and don't try to dominate the team."

—Female Student

We all have had experiences with individuals engaged in these negative practices and most likely have participated in them, as well. Under- and over-functioning team members have the potential to hurt themselves and others. Learning to be responsible for self is a vital and necessary part of growth in relationship to the Lord and to others.

And yet we must also realize that, for various reasons, some difficult people are not willing or able to make the necessary changes. Some will never achieve responsibility for self, but we may have to learn to accept them as they are and work with them anyway. So how does a group go about dealing with these difficult situations? The answer is at once profoundly simple and incredibly complex: by living and acting in the grace of God. In their focus groups, students often mentioned grace as an important element in developing meaningful partnership.

6. Giving Grace to All

Just two years ago, I was asked to speak on the "gravity of grace" in chapel at my university. The timing couldn't have been worse. I was really struggling to keep going that semester. I would finish one task and discover four more that I had missed. Sluggish, forgetful, and unfocused, I struggled to come up with something meaningful to say. And if my personal struggles weren't enough of a challenge, the thought of speaking to a large daily assembly of college students more occupied with cell phones, text messages, studying, laughing, talking, and even sneezing in ways that distract was close to overwhelming.

The night before the presentation I woke up at 1:25 a.m. in a cold sweat from a nightmare about my chapel speech. In the dream, I was coming down from the top of our school's coliseum, where we hold daily chapel, to get to the stage. I had already been introduced so everyone was watching me struggle to come down the steps. Instead of making a graceful appearance on the stage, I fell down a long flight of stairs with the entire student body watching. Now it would be tempting to laugh this experience off and say "it was only a nightmare," but I have exhibited my clumsiness far too often to dismiss it. I fell going up the stairs in chapel while I was a student at the same college, displaying more than I ever meant to as my skirt flew up. Another time, I fell off the jogging trampoline in our living room and tore the ligaments in my left ankle. For weeks, people asked me if the bandage and crutches were from skiing. I so wanted to say "yes." But the truth is, I am simply a klutz.

My physical life in so many ways parallels my spiritual. I am not naturally a graceful person; I am often struggling, sluggish, forgetful, and unfocused. I speak when I should listen, move forward when I should wait, and form judgments without knowing all I should. Fortunately, God is not waiting for me to get my act together, God has already provided all the grace we need. But I don't always live with this truth in mind.

Too many of us are quick to see difficult people as persons to avoid, troubled situations as something to "handle," instead of recognizing moments of conflict as God-given times when grace is abundantly present and operative. Grace isn't what I once thought it was: I do the best that I can and then God makes up the difference. Grace covers everything. God in Christ went to the depths of hell and the heights of heaven to make known the love, grace, and power that is possible through Jesus. That is what the Lord's life, death, burial, and resurrection are all about. We live in the assurance that there is "nothing in this world that can separate us from the love of God in Christ Jesus" (Rom. 8:31–39). Yet as we begin to understand this great truth, we are tempted to ask the infamous question: If grace covers me for everything then I can just keep on doing whatever I want, can't I?

Anticipating this response, the apostle Paul writes in Romans 6:15, "What then? Should we sin because we are not under law but under grace? By no means!" Paul further instructs readers to live lives that reflect the great grace we have been given, issuing this appeal to himself and others: "by the mercies of God, [let us] present our bodies as living sacrifices, holy and acceptable to God which is our spiritual worship" (12:1). What exactly does this all mean, and how does it apply to the formation of godly partnership between men and women?

Presenting ourselves as living sacrifices means that we continually surrender upon the altar of God, willing to give up everything. It is only through this reality that we are able to live resurrected lives. In this state, we realize that whatever circumstances we find ourselves in as Christians, we can know that God will give us the help and strength, the courage and faith to do exactly what is required. Death is never easy, resurrection is impossible—and yet we live in the mystery of both because of who God is and what God has done. This truth means that we should live, think, and act from a position of grace.

We recognize that we too are difficult to live with, that we present challenges for others working for us, and that we want others to be gracious to us when we are. Acknowledging this reality and confessing our failures both help us learn to be gracious toward others, as we have opened the door for them to be gracious toward us. It also helps us to be gracious toward ourselves. Often the person who is hardest on me is me. But if I live in grace I must extend it everywhere, even to myself. Walking in grace is a choice that we make. Yes, God extends grace to everyone, but not everyone chooses to accept it. God never forces us to be obedient, never insists that we accept what is offered. Rather, God gives us free will and allows us to choose to be in the Lord, or not. Sometimes in our attempts to help others, we forget that they also have the freedom of choice, and we cannot choose for them. In the context of partnership, that means that we can pray for others, walk faithfully beside them, encourage them to make good decisions, and hold them accountable in the process. It also means that we can offer support and love them whatever decisions they make. But through it all, we remember that choices are theirs just as much as ours. The only person I can ever change is me.

Probably my favorite class period with our majors was the final one. Here they received the final grades for their service-learning projects. Some of the feedback came from the three professors, some from the service-providers with whom they worked, and, of course, some from other members of the team. We presented the focus group data, and they were able to see the larger picture of the projects and the formation of their partnerships. As they met for the last time with their learning teams, students either spoke honestly about unresolved issues or abandoned them all together. I could hear words of encouragement and apology throughout the room. It was a time for laughter, sharing, tears, and prayers.

These women and men formed partnerships, journeyed together, learned about one another and themselves, and served those in need. They told their stories, kept a covenant with each other, experienced various forms of leadership, learned to take responsibility for self, and, I believe, extended grace abundantly. My prayer for them has always been that they learned the importance of their work together, as men and women, for the whole community of faith. It is exciting to participate with God in the formation of these ministers in whatever context they choose to serve. I cannot wait to see how God continues to work in their lives and partnerships.

Thoughts on Working Together

"Because of the troubles we experienced, I have truly realized that as a team, no matter what is going on, you have to be completely honest with each other about things that could affect your work together as a team. Our team has great relationships that were already strong before our team came together, but because we did not communicate well, we did not achieve the set goal."

—Male Student

Conclusion

What began as a simple experiment in a social gathering early in our marriage has become the norm for Jack and me. We still love to "mix it up" and get out of our comfort zones. To be with those who are different from me can be challenging but also very enriching. Whether he knew it or not, Jack was setting an important agenda that night with his simple decision. Each of our adult children has expressed appreciation for what they have learned growing up in a home that valued diversity and experimentation.

We each, of course, enjoy plenty of time with friends and colleagues of our same genders. I have been with the same Bunko group for many years and have served for a decade in a worldwide ministry by women for women to support and encourage missionaries and national leaders. A significant part of my job description at Abilene Christian University centers around working with young women. Likewise Jack regularly meets with, prays with, and even enjoys fishing with different groups of men. But we also love and appreciate the many mixed gender groups that we get to participate in.

Analyzing my students' responses in working with each other these past several years has deeply enriched my life. Identifying the importance of story delighted me since, as I already confessed, I love to hear and tell stories. Yet now I have a more focused purpose in telling my story and hearing others—forming greater partnerships.

Learning the importance of finding our centers of identity has also significantly affected my perspective on relationships. In many of our conversations, we tend to take the principle of putting God first and loving our neighbor second and apply it only to our individual lives. Seeing this as an important element of godly partnership allowed me to recognize the urgency of making this application corporately.

Observing the need for better communication in student groups made it possible for me to see this element through more spiritual eyes and, therefore, gave me a whole new framework from which to grow.

Considering when to step up and when to step down not only enabled me to discover types of leaderships found in each group, but also challenged me to examine leadership in the many partnerships in which I serve. Establishing more awareness about when to rise up and fall back has been especially meaningful to my own development as a leader.

Finally, watching the groups opened my eyes to the value of taking responsibility for self and giving grace to all. Some of the groups focused on the importance of making sacrifices, others on the need for respect. Naturally, many students were frustrated by their teammates and their work within each group. Yet in discussing how to respond in order to achieve godly partnership, these two areas seemed to capture every frustration presented and the suggestions students gave for addressing them.

My family, colleagues, and students were so patient and generous throughout the process of this partnership experiment. I hope the things we accomplished and lessons we learned can help you, and all people partnering together, as we all continue to work toward more effective and enlivening relationships.

Chapter Four

Nurturing Partnership
Why the Church Must Lead the Way

Beginning a new ministry is both invigorating and frightening, especially if the whole context is unfamiliar. Jack and I had just moved with our three children to Memphis where Jack would be teaching at a seminary after several years of preaching. While still struggling to adjust, we were hired to serve half-time as co-directors of the singles ministry at one of the larger churches in town.

Our first Monday on the job, we walked into the staff meeting ready to get acquainted and learn more about the congregation and how it functioned. Everyone greeted us warmly. After a few minutes of visiting, Harold, the senior minister, turned to me and asked if I would lead the group in prayer.

I was momentarily taken aback, because the prevailing Southern culture and normal polity of our church fellowship did not allow for women to lead prayers in public settings. But I found enough composure to pray, and then Harold began the meeting with a welcome and introduction. Harold described what the church had in mind in starting this new ministry. He also told the staff that he wanted it to be clear that both Jack and I were working in this ministry and were therefore equal partners. And he lived up to his word.

From the moment we joined that congregation we were welcomed as valued colleagues and gifted ministers. We were only part-time, and I was among the first women to be hired as a minister, yet the staff, church leadership, and congregants were respectful, affirming, and encouraging. Partnerships flourished on numerous fronts.

The situation was not without difficulties, of course. We were new to this church, new to the surrounding culture, and new to this particular ministry. Many accommodations had to be made on all fronts. Jack felt encouraged there, but I especially blossomed because I felt secure, valued, and loved. Our short period of time there made a great difference in my formation as a minister and especially as a partner. I am thankful to that church and others that have shown me not only how significant partnerships are formed but also how they are nurtured.

Within the church, numerous partnerships exist: between appointed leadership and paid ministerial staff, between ministers and lay leaders, ministers and members, lay leaders and volunteers, and so on. In some congregations, these partnerships flourish and grow, in others they flounder and die. Why? What is the difference in churches that bless and nurture partnerships and those that don't? I will explore the qualities these churches possess toward the end of this chapter.

Before we go there, however, I want to do a basic examination of culture, discuss how Christians often respond to it, consider God's relationship with culture, and explore how all of these potentially impact our understanding of partnership. I am firmly convinced that the church, fully engaged with the prevailing culture, must lead the way in establishing and supporting godly partnerships between women and men. To do so requires that we have thoughtful conversation with Scripture and culture in order to know how to interact effectively with both. To do anything else is to ignore not only how we are shaped by culture, but also how we influence it.

Brief Overview of Culture

Culture is the word anthropologists use to describe the structured customs and underlying worldview assumptions by which people govern their lives. All people are products of their culture. It is what shapes life and gives it meaning. People learn culture, however; it is not transmitted genetically. Each society has a body of learned behaviors, images, values, and constructs that are transmitted from generation to generation and become a template by which people, in any particular context, cope with their physical and social environments. These learned assumptions form an individual's worldview and deeply affect how one thinks, feels, and acts. As Charles H. Kraft writes,

> A culture may be likened to a river, with a surface level and a deep level. The surface is visible. Most of the river, however, lies beneath the surface, and is largely invisible. But anything that happens on the surface of the river is affected by such deep-level phenomena as the current, the cleanness or dirtiness of the river, other objects in the river and so on. What happens on the surface of a river is both a response to external phenomena and a manifestation of the deep-level characteristics of the river.[1]

Much of the time we are content to stay at the surface level of culture and think that we know a particular group of people and their values. We even approach our own culture this way. Anyone who has ever lived and worked in another culture, however, will tell you that it is not until we begin to know and understand the deeper levels of a culture and its people that we are really interacting significantly with them.

Thoughts on Working Together

"Overall our group worked really well together and I think we were all satisfied with the way things turned out. We like each other well enough, and we always can find something to talk about. Also, when there was tension we did not let it become the center of what was happening or let it control our emotions. When it comes to my personal struggle with conflict, I decided to not let people run over me or change my view by their attitude. Usually, if a person takes an opposite view in an abrasive tone, I start stumbling all over myself to try to make what I just said more towards their way of thinking. I do not like that I do this and have noticed it more as I get older. I usually do not stick up for my own beliefs as being valid enough as I should. This semester I voiced my opinions more but I also did not get so uptight about how things were supposed to go."

—Female Student

I recently attended an adult Sunday school class where the teacher spent a great deal of time explaining why Christians must abandon everything about the world around us and simply live for Jesus. I sat there wondering how it was possible to do such a thing. I agree with the teacher that Christ calls us to live a whole new way of life, but we always do that *within* the context of our culture. From its beginning, the church has always had to come to grips with its place within culture. No matter where I go or what I do, I cannot escape the fact that my culture shapes me. To think otherwise is to allow cultural influences to go unexamined, thus giving them more power in my life. In each time and place of history, in every social and familial situation, God's will and purpose for humanity must be both realized (that we will live the life of faith) and reinterpreted (what it looks like in this context). Yet this task is not an easy one and historically has yielded varying responses from people of faith.

Culture forms our understanding of gender, so central to our identity as human beings, and how men and women function with each other and in society. Mary Stewart Van Leeuwen writes, "Culture is the crucible in which all human development takes place."[2] Yet Christians have not always had an easy relationship with culture and its influence upon us. Too often, we have avoided cultural influences, tried to alter the culture itself, or acted as if cultural norms should be embraced without question. These decisions inevitably contribute to our understanding of both culture and ourselves, determining how we view both men and women as individuals and as partners with one another.

Christian Responses to Culture

Rejecting culture. Those who choose to reject culture's influence in shaping their lives tend to fall along a spectrum. Most extreme are Christians who deny all outside culture. This response is the traditional one of separatists who believe the culture is irredeemable and contact with it must be avoided at all cost. Our years in Iowa brought us into closer contact with the Amish. Their tight-knit communities, well-kept farms, and quiet, respectful demeanor impressed us deeply. Yet few would deny that their response to culture is extreme—they see it as something to be completely avoided. Members live isolated from others, avoiding modern conveniences and mass media.

Less radical in the culture-rejecting category are Christians who "ignore the culture." These individuals often assume that whatever is presented in popular culture is trivial or unimportant. It has no affect on Bible-believing Christians and should be simply disregarded. I have friends who feel that because they are Christian that they cannot watch television, attend a popular movie, or read a current bestseller—these things have too much potential to corrupt, and so they simply avoid them.

These Christians' focus on purity and simplicity is admirable and shapes many of the choices they make for themselves and their children as they work to create alternate, more wholesome, cultures in their homes. Home schooling as an educational option, for example, has grown in strength and in quality over the past several years in large part as a result of parents who want to maximize Christian influences and minimize secular ones for their families.

Altering culture. Another overarching approach to culture is found among Christians who believe their responsibility is to alter it. This "change the culture" view historically was the domain of theological liberals or social activists. However, beginning in the late 1970s, the American theological right began to stress this approach. Any political campaign in recent years provides evidence of this shift. Many conservative Christians rally behind candidates because of their views on issues such as abortion, same-sex marriage, and prayer in schools. Such strength of conviction is commendable until it becomes a test of orthodoxy and those who hold different opinions are considered suspect.

Closely related to people who seek to change the culture are those who "manipulate it." These individuals take cultural elements and Christianize them. In essence they create a whole new reality filled with Christian music, Christian movies, Christian fiction, Christian Web sites, Christian dating services, and so on. The financial success of the Christian market is evident of this approach's popularity.

Appreciating culture. Finally, we must look at Christians who seem to appreciate culture, though they manifest it in dramatically different ways. First are those who choose to "debate the culture." They tend to study both the social role and the content of mass media in order to know how to respond to it. They learn to work within the institutions that shape culture in order to know how to challenge it more effectively. Often known as the missionary approach, individuals in this category are able to bring the gospel to others but sometimes experience alienation and even persecution in doing so. Second are Christians who seek to "baptize the culture." This response is most often identified with the religious left and holds that culture is often ahead of the church in its understanding of human rights and related issues. Many people who lean in this direction believe the church should grow with and even follow culture in seeking truth.

This last view is the polar opposite of those who try to separate themselves from culture. Together these show the two extremes to which Christians sometimes go in dealing with culture—making culture our enemy or finding ourselves in bed with it. All of our difficulties with culture, however, originate in our failure to see that God created culture and rules over all cultures.

God and Culture

When the Lord tells the newly created man and woman: "Be fruitful and multiply, and fill the earth and subdue it; and have dominion over the fish of the sea and over the birds of the air and over every living thing that moves upon the earth" (Gen. 1:28), God forms the first culture. Even after sin alters life in the garden and humanity is expelled from it, God continues to be involved with creating culture. At Babel, as people decide to build a city with a tower to the heavens and amass power for themselves, God foils their plans and divides them into various people groups with different languages and eventually varying values, traditions, and worldviews (Gen. 11:6–9).

It is tempting here to see varied cultures as the result of human vanity and desire for power instead of part of God's design for the world. However, if God were not pleased with the rich diversity of cultures that still exists, then I think Pentecost would have gone differently. When the Spirit was poured out on the apostles, those present heard the gospel in their own tongues (Acts 2:5–12). God did not choose to reunite human speech and reverse the effects of Babel but rather united humanity through the proclamation of the gospel. Even in John's apocalyptic revelation, the gospel was proclaimed "to those who live on the earth—to every nation and tribe and language and people" (Rev. 14:6).

Finally, Scripture makes it clear that God rules over all cultures. Paul writes to the Romans that Christians should be subject "to the governing authorities; for there is no authority except from God, and those authorities that exist have been instituted by God" (Rom. 13:1ff). Again, Christians in Asia Minor were instructed to "accept the authority of every human institution whether of the emperor as supreme, or of governors, as sent by him to punish those who do wrong and to praise those who do right" (1 Pet. 2:13–14). Exactly what these commands mean in varying situations has mystified Christians for centuries. My intention is not to unpack and apply them widely but to allow us to see God's involvement with, and authority over, all culture.

Thoughtful Engagement with Culture

A growing trend emerging from several corners of the Christian community calls believers to critically engage culture by asking difficult questions of it without compromising their faith. This view calls us away from either rejecting culture or overvaluing it. It allows us to relate to people and our environment yet live in the tension of being different. It affirms the countercultural nature of the Christian faith found in 1 Peter. There, the writer acknowledges that Christians must persevere in their faith even though the world around them not only misunderstands but also possibly persecutes them. This courageous way of living may appeal to or repulse non-Christians, but it is challenging and rewarding for believers. It calls for a great deal of wisdom, discernment, and sacrifice as we live out faith in a troubled world.

Tying all this back to our discussion of how we partner with one another as women and men, we realize that all of our cultures carry expectations about gender and relationships that have shaped us. Therefore, the responses to culture we choose matter. It matters that I recognize my cultural context and how it has formed me as a person and a part of a community. It matters not only for my understanding of what it means to be a woman, but for also how I relate to others and vice versa. It matters because it informs how I see gender roles and expectations. It matters because I bring my culture, my understanding of it, my response to it, and all that I am to my Christian walk.

If I primarily see culture as an enemy to be avoided, changed, or manipulated, then it would not be surprising that I reject current trends of how women and men interact with one another. Christians who choose these responses often hold to more hierarchical, patriarchal views of gender relationships. Men hold public, leadership positions and women do not, though they are often respected and appreciated in different ways. The primary sphere of influence for women is with other women and children. The function of each gender is considered complementary to the other with distinct masculine and feminine characteristics. Mary Stewart Van Leeuwen describes complementarity in "Opposite Sexes or Neighboring Sexes?" by drawing on John Gray's familiar *Men are from Mars, Women are from Venus* metaphor, saying,

> [Many share] a common desire to defend the concept of "gender complementarity": roughly, the notion that "men and women are different." This gets expressed in different ways—most crudely by some who insist that men and women have completely dichotomous and fixed psychological traits. (Call this, if you will, the "Men are from Mars, women are from Venus" stance—with or without the planetary terminology.) More common, but only slightly more nuanced, is the acknowledgment by some in both camps that male-female personality and behavioral differences (e.g., in aggression, in relational skills) are "general" or "average"

differences only, not absolute differences. This, however, is still seen to count as "gender complementarity." (Call this, if you will, the "*Most* men are from Mars and *most* women are from Venus *most* of the time" stance).[3]

Partnership from this vantage point is possible but with definite boundaries and limitations.

If I assume a more amenable response toward culture, seeing it as something to be appreciated, even embraced, then I am freer to adopt a broader view of how men and women work together. In today's democratic society in the United States, it is not surprising that our culture makes equality a high priority. If we adopt this viewpoint, men and women are able to function in any role within the church without discrimination. Complementarity is still a high priority, but without as many boundaries and limitations as in a model that wholly denies the value of our culture.

Two problems exist with either of these positions, however. First, both tend to assume that the understanding they hold of gender is immutable and, therefore, should be accepted as the norm. Those who are hierarchical may see distinct roles for men and for women, while those who are egalitarian may believe we should never make distinctions. Second, both positions appeal to the social sciences for support and read their understanding back into Scripture. Van Leeuwen reports, however, that current research simply does not indicate differences in the sexes that many assume.[4] Neither does careful exegesis of relevant passages in Scripture lead to clearcut understanding about gender roles. Therefore, since both camps believe decisions about how men and women function have already been determined and that changing gender identity is destructive or impossible, neither of these views actually allows us to critically engage culture or Scripture. The irony is that while both positions think they foster healthy and godly partnerships, they hold great potential to inhibit the formation and growth of such relationships.

If we are to live counterculturally, we must assume a learning stance toward both the world we live in and the Bible that guides us. Churches that foster such a stance are more likely to develop meaningful partnership and serve as beacons of light to the world around them. I have observed a few of these qualities and would like to explore them here. I am confident that readers will be able to identify even more characteristics not mentioned, but my intention is to begin the conversation in some churches and further it in others, while also continuing to develop my own understanding of and growth in partnership.

Thoughts on Working Together

"Churches need to be more service-oriented in their actions. When people serve together, God brings them together in ways unimaginable otherwise. Ministry staffs and elderships should make service a regular activity to create team cohesiveness."

—Male Student

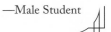

Churches That Lead the Way

Communities of faith that seek to engage the surrounding culture and empower women and men to serve together are not afraid to ask difficult questions of the text, of their culture, and of themselves. They examine and re-examine Scripture closely to determine how to apply it in their particular times and places. They interact with culture to find out both the needs of those around them and where God is already at work in the world. They scrutinize their own lives to see where God might be leading them and what gifts they have to serve and bless others.

They live like pioneers settling new territory, always anticipating what adventures as well as what dangers lie ahead. They live with hope, courage, faith, and confidence, seeking God's preferred future for their communities. These churches exhibit at least the following five perspectives.

1. *These churches understand that timing is everything.* Our family members say to one another frequently, "timing is everything." It is meant to give us pause, to buy time to think and reconsider. Or we use it to inform each other that a better moment might make it possible for us to really be heard. Too frequently, we do not pay enough attention to timing. We either forge ahead to take care of something, or we wait too long and miss valuable opportunities. But God does not make decisions as we do.

Rather, God has perfect timing. So when Gabriel is instructed by God to visit the young unmarried virgin Mary, God has planned the moment and the message carefully (Luke 1:26–38). God is breaking into history in a way that, although prophesied about, was not understood fully until after Jesus' death. Jesus comes to the earth into a specific context—he is born into a Jewish family and reared in the Jewish faith.

Throughout his public ministry, Jesus refers to a sense of timing that comes from the Father. For example, as the disciples are about to celebrate the festival of Booths, Jesus instructs them, "My time has not yet come, but your time is always here. The world cannot hate you, but it hates me because I testify against it that its works are evil. Go to the festival yourselves. I am not going to this festival, for my time has not yet fully come" (John 7:6–8). In other places in John's gospel, Jesus speaks of an appointed hour (7:30; 12:23, 27; 16:32) that is clearly associated with his death, burial, and resurrection.

What also becomes clear in Jesus' life and ministry, his crucifixion and resurrection, is that his ministry is not limited to the Jews. Although Jesus' earthly context was Jewish, his purpose included possible salvation for all. God's perfect timing also reflects God's perfect love for the whole world (John 3:16).

For Christians interested in participating in God's work in the world, so many elements affect how we approach it. We realize that we live in a specific context. It is not a small thing for our churches to follow Christ's example in knowing not only *who* we are, but also *when* and *where* we are. Our purpose in being God's people at this time and this place, whatever that might be, allows us to think about the cultural moment in which we find ourselves and to live the gospel there.

The truth is, we must pay attention to these matters, or the church will not be a vibrant and living community for the next generation. Our teenage and adult children are begging us to stop arguing over what they consider insignificant issues while people around us go hungry and cannot find meaningful work. Many of our churches already are losing their young people in great numbers—I hear it everywhere I go. But these young people are not leaving the faith, just the institutional church. They are looking for communities that will be on the frontlines, working shoulder to shoulder, women and men, across racial, ethnic, and economic divides, all of us together to serve the needs and to bring the good news to those who need it most—the least of these. Such a commitment is why God sent Jesus into the world and why God sends us out as well.

2. *They wait for the Spirit.* A word that I have never liked and one I have struggled to live with at times: *wait.* So often, however, it is the word from the Lord for us. The instruction comes when we anticipate something really wonderful about to happen, when we are in the middle of a crisis and need help, or when we are challenged to make a decision and the timing seems urgent. *Wait.* "Wait? Lord that's not really an answer," I want to cry. *Wait?!* "But we're running out of time, the deadline is looming," we want to remind God. *Wait.* "Wait for what Lord? I don't have enough patience to wait." And yet waiting is all too often the only response given.

Wait was the instruction Jesus gave followers at his ascension. And so they left Olivet and returned to Jerusalem and went to an upstairs room. A small group gathered, including the apostles, Jesus' mother Mary, and Jesus' brothers (Acts 1:12–14). So what were they waiting for? Jesus told them to wait until they received "power when the Holy Spirit has come upon you; and you will be my witnesses in Jerusalem, in all Judea and Samaria, and to the ends of the earth" (1:8). And so they waited.

Most of us, however, know the rest of the story. We know that on the day of Pentecost, they were once again gathered and heard the rush of a violent wind from heaven that filled the entire house where they were. Tongues like fire appeared among them and a tongue rested on each of them. "All were filled with the Holy Spirit and began to speak in other languages as the Spirit gave them ability" (Acts 2:1–4).

I have often heard reference made to Peter's preaching of Joel 2 about the Spirit being poured out on old and young, male and female, enslaved and free. But as a child I was also taught that only the apostles (that is, the men) had the gift of tongues for preaching. That is not how the text reads. Those who were gathered, those who had waited, all received the empowerment of the Spirit as Jesus had promised. Three thousand people were baptized that day, receiving forgiveness of their sins and the gift of the Holy Spirit.

We no longer have to wait for the outpouring of God's Spirit—it has been, is being, and will continue to be accomplished. Churches that recognize the Spirit in all their members will more naturally be inclined to look for and use the gifts given to each one. In fact, Ephesians 4 seems to indicate that the gifts are not actually given to specific individuals but rather these gifted people are given to the church for the good of all. The gifts are given "to equip the saints for the work of ministry, for building up the body of Christ" for promoting our growth in unity and maturity (4:12–13).

In Spirit-filled churches, partnerships are able to form without concern over issues of gender, age, race, or status. Members enrich community life by their involvement in various combinations of ministry. Each member is valued as a person whom God has saved, sanctified, and empowered for the good of the Kingdom. Members use wisdom and discernment to help others determine their gifts and how they might bless others. Prayer is a constant activity in these churches and maturity is a natural outgrowth. Just as the first disciples who received the Spirit began to spread the good news and meet the needs of one another, so women and men today who are filled with the Spirit will work effectively together toward the same purposes.

3. *They recognize the importance of prayer.* The whole church was stricken at the news: Doris was admitted to the hospital in grave condition. The doctor gave her only a fifty percent chance of survival, and that was because he was a strong Christian. Immediately cards, letters, phone calls, and casseroles began to circulate. Paul, her husband, was a beloved and respected elder of the church. Doris was harder to describe. She was active in working with all children and teenagers. She was no bigger than an average ten year old herself, and it was not uncommon to find her in the middle of a large crowd of young people everywhere she went. People all over town knew and loved her. Everyone wanted her to recover, and the sooner, the better. (Our three children were at the top of that list.)

Jack and I had served this congregation for five years, he as the preacher and I as a leader of the women's ministry. Just a few weeks earlier, we informed the elders that we were leaving that summer for Jack to go into academics. The decision to go had been very difficult—something we prayed about not only for the sake of our family and future careers but also because of where we were in relation to the church. Although many good things happened during our tenure there, we somehow did not feel that our work was complete. And then Doris got sick.

The waiting room of the intensive care unit was crammed full of individuals anxious to see how Paul and Doris were doing. People kept asking what they could do, and others kept responding, "All we can do now is pray." Have you ever thought about how we make that statement in desperate times? All we can do now is pray. It makes prayer seem like a last resort, as if we are resigned to a great inactivity that keeps us occupied, rather than the first step we should take in any situation. But at this time, the church really prayed.

Members set up prayer vigils at the hospital, with a team always present praying for the doctors, the nurses, and, of course, Doris and her family. The church held prayer meetings three times a day—morning, noon, and night—at the church building. People who could not be present at either of these were asked to keep prayer watches in their homes and were scheduled for prayer slots around the clock. We prayed, and prayed, and prayed for over a week. Men and women, young and old, strangers and close friends—we prayed like we had never prayed before.

That Sunday morning when Jack stood up to preach, he simply could not offer any words of wisdom or even comfort. Doris' condition remained the same. So eight hundred Christians dropped to their knees in prayer. The prayer that morning was more fervent and intense than I had ever heard. At that point, we did not know what God would do for Doris and Paul, but we certainly knew that God was changing the hearts of this group of Christians. God accomplished in that two-week period what Jack and I had hoped for and worked toward for the past five years.

Doris recovered. She lived for several more years and she and Paul continued their faithful service to many. Since that time the congregation has grown and flourished immeasurably; today, they are a healthy, vibrant, growing church. Jack and I, and our kids, were sad to leave that summer—we loved this body of believers—but we also left with gratitude, because this congregation was made up of a changed people. God used what seemed to be a crisis in our collective lives to bring us to our knees in humility, earnestness, and faith. We went from being a group of people who said, "all we can do now is pray," to a church who knew prayer was the first and best activity we could undertake. I always wondered if Doris knew how God used her to change a whole community of faith.

4. *They value unity in diversity.* Imagine a gathering of the early church. I think of it this way: The host and hostess would welcome all who came and invite them into their home. Each person would bring an offering—perhaps a significant portion of the common meal or maybe just a single fish or loaf of bread. Others would sell property and bring the proceeds to share, while some might offer only a coin or two. The group would consist of an odd mixture of people, hardly those who would socialize with one another in the ancient world—Jews and Gentiles, rich and poor, slaves and masters, men and women, children and the aged. They worshipped the Lord with songs, prayers, and readings.

Those attending spoke words of encouragement and exhortation. Occasionally they would have word from one of the apostles or a traveling evangelist. The evening would culminate in a common meal, part of which celebrated Jesus' death, burial, and resurrection and gave them hope to continue living in a world hostile to their faith. They would leave carrying various offerings to those who could not come for worship or those who were in need.

Never before had people from such diverse backgrounds and different socio-economic levels found common ground in their faith. This incredible unity in the midst of such diversity was quite evident in the first churches but it was certainly not without problems. Read any of Paul's letters to various churches and you will see hints of disunity, disharmony, and disagreement.

None is more apparent than in the discord in Corinth. They were divided over which leaders were the greatest, how to conduct themselves sexually, who should settle legal disputes, whether they could eat meat sacrificed to idols, how women should serve in public ministry, and which spiritual gifts were the greatest. (And we think we've got new troubles in our congregations today.)

The apostle faithfully addresses each of these concerns and calls them to two radically Christian ideals. The first is a reminder that they are one body: "For just as the body is one and has many members, and all the members of the body, though many, are one body, so it is with Christ. For in the one Spirit we are all baptized into one body—Jews or Greeks, slaves or free—and we were all to drink of one Spirit" (1 Cor. 12:12–13). Paul further explains that no part of the body can say to another that it is not needed. He reminds them, and us, "God arranged the members in the body, each one of them, as God chose" (12:18).

All parts of the body are needed and valued and must be cared for. Paul reminds the Corinthians that if one part of the body suffers, the whole body suffers; if one member is honored, then all celebrate (12:26). God designed the church, like the physical body, to include widely differing members who are interdependent and unified in purpose. Churches that understand Paul's message about unity in diversity are more likely to foster meaningful and godly partnerships.

Paul's second radical ideal for Christians is that love trumps everything else. It is the spiritual gift given to all. It is the gift that shows fullness of life lived in Christ and the rich possibilities of our being together. Love allows adherents to be patient, kind, sacrificial, empathetic, and considerate of others—all qualities needed for members of the body to live and work in partnership. And best of all, love never ends nor does the potential for our growth and maturation in it. Imagine partnerships flourishing in churches like these.

5. *They handle conflict well.* The church at Philippi knew a lot about love. Many readers consider Paul's correspondence to this young congregation a love letter because of the numerous statements of affection he makes in it (1:7, 12; 2:12; 4:1, 8). It is also a book about partnership. Paul sees this church as his partner in the gospel (1:5, 14; 4:3, 15). Yet reading the whole epistle, one sees hints that all is not well, conflict is brewing just

under the surface, and the apostle wants to keep it from erupting into something more critical.

The first hint comes in chapter one, where Paul prays that their love may overflow with "knowledge and full insight" (1:9–11). He challenges them to look out for the interests of others, not just their own (2:4) and to not murmur or argue as they live together (2:14–15). In chapter four, he specifically challenges two women, Euodia and Syntyche, to "be of the same mind in the Lord" (4:2).

Throughout the epistle, Paul exhorts Christians, then and now, that only one thing really matters: that they live their lives "in a manner worthy of the gospel of Christ" (1:27). To live with this perspective, according to Paul, is to stand firm together without being intimidated by those who would oppose them. Paul sees the inevitable suffering that comes with this kind of stance as equal to the privilege of believing in Christ (1:30). What enables believers to live in this type of radical unity is the sacrifice that Jesus made in humbling himself and becoming obedient to the point of death (2:6–11). Paul cites examples throughout Philippians of those who live sacrificially for the sake of others: Timothy, Epaphroditus, and even himself. It is only from the position of having counted everything he'd gained as loss (3:7–11) that Paul is able to stand faithfully with other believers and to demand that all Christians follow suit.

What becomes clear in this letter is that part of living out the Gospel is being able to stand with others, even when we disagree with them. Paul calls us to rejoice, to be gentle, to not worry, and to be thankful in prayer (4:4–6). Furthermore, we are to guard our thoughts, focusing only on good things and following the examples of those who live likewise, knowing that the God of peace will be with us (4:8–9).

Philippians helps us to see that in churches, even those in which members love each other deeply, conflict is inevitable. Working with one another in partnership for the gospel does not free us from conflict.

Instead, it infuses us with a desire to develop a plan for resolving it and a purpose in holding one another accountable to that plan.

Through my observations and experiences I have found these five attributes—understanding that timing is everything, waiting for the Spirit, recognizing the importance of prayer, valuing unity in diversity, and handling conflict well—are found in many healthy, thriving congregations. It is not surprising that when I speak to members of these churches, they report a high level of satisfaction with the spiritual nourishment they receive. It is not surprising that many individuals in these churches are involved in meaningful ministries that meet the needs of those in their community. It is not surprising that outsiders seem drawn to such vibrant churches. And it is not surprising that partnership in ministry between men and women is highly valued and encouraged in these faith communities.

So how does a congregation go about becoming such a leading church? The first step is to ask difficult questions of Scripture and to pray about what we discover there. Christians should never be afraid to reconsider any former interpretations or to discover whole new insights in the text. At the same time, prayer must be a central activity. Setting up prayer vigils, prayer teams, and prayer retreats are a few simple measures that can dramatically change the life of a church. We must also pay attention to direction from the Spirit, both in the congregation and in the surrounding area. Too often we assume that God is only at work in those who claim to be followers. Yet when we have eyes to see, we will discern the Spirit's movement in unexpected forms, in unexpected places, and within unexpected people.

Will these activities cause conflict in our midst? Yes—and we should welcome that conflict. Which churches in the New Testament had no conflict? The Corinthians? The Galatians? The Thessalonians? They were as filled with conflict as the church at Philippi. Our question should not be, how we can avoid conflict? but rather, how we can handle it well?

How, in the name of Jesus, can our communities of faith live together with all the diversity and challenges we face and still be faithful witnesses and godly servants in the world?

Thoughts on Working Together

"Partnership in ministry implies that the partners show up ready to serve or work. Partners need to work with each other side-by-side at some point in their ministry so they can share the same struggles and hardships. One of the main components of making a team work well together is the camaraderie the players gain by struggling through two-a-day practices together. People who are partners in ministry go through rough times together to gain a mutual respect for each other. I think this is especially true for women in ministry. I feel that I have had to work twice as hard in ministry situations to gain respect, especially from my male partners."

—Female Student

My prayer is that we will realize that the time is now. Christians are uniquely positioned to engage our culture in meaningful ways. I pray that we will not miss the opportunities presented to us. As the Civil Rights movement emerged in the 50s and grew into the 60s, too few Christians were found on the front lines. Too many chose to turn their faces from the racial inequities evident throughout our culture. Too many moved from the city to the suburbs to avoid living in racially diverse neighborhoods. Too many left integrated public schools and founded private Christian schools instead. These choices left a stain on Christianity. I pray that we will not repeat the mistakes of the past in relation to gender issues. As faithful women and men, we need to lead the culture and the church in understanding the significance of godly partnership to fulfill God's purposes in the world.

Conclusion

The opportunity Jack and I had to serve in a shared ministry didn't last long. We struggled to decide whether we would stay there or take the opportunity for him to teach at our alma mater. We knew that there were definite advantages and disadvantages to whichever direction we chose. Moving back to Texas meant we could be closer to family and expanded ministry opportunities for Jack. But what would I do? Could I find meaningful ministry? Would we be able to work together again?

After a few months in which Jack served as interim minister in a couple of congregations, we still had not found a church home. Honestly, we were looking for a place where our family could be fed but also where I might find employment. The latter possibilities were very limited.

One evening we were enjoying a meal with good friends and sharing our concerns and difficulties in these areas. One of these friends, David, turned to me and asked, "What is your vision of your ministry, Jeanene? What do you see yourself doing in the future?" I told him that I did not have such a vision nor any certainty about what it would be now or in the future. He said he found my answer odd, since he saw me as a visionary person. I told him that I had not dared dream about ministry but chose rather to take what was available.

"Why?" he asked.

"Because I love the church," was my response. "And I have never wanted to be disappointed with it or critical of it."

We closed the evening in prayer but it was as if a door to my heart had been opened, and I did not know what to think or do about it. Eventually, I discovered that I did have a vision of how I wanted to serve God and others—through preparing young men and women for ministry.

I pursued my advanced degrees and joined Jack and others in teaching in the College of Biblical Studies at Abilene Christian University.

But part of my response to David's question remains true. I do love the church, and I still do not want to be disappointed with it or critical of it. I hope that this chapter has demonstrated these sentiments. I pray that we have been challenged to think more creatively about culture, our involvement with it, and ways in which we can promote fuller lives of faith for all our members.

Notes to Chapter Four

1. Charles H. Kraft, "Culture, Worldview and Contextualization," in *Perspectives: On the World Christian Movement,* Ralph D. Winter and Steven C. Hawthorne, eds. (Pasadena: William Carey Library, 1999), 385.

2. Mary Stewart Van Leeuwen, *Gender and Grace: Love, Work, and Parenting in a Changing World* (Downers Grove: InterVarsity, 1990), 109.

3. Mary Stewart Van Leeuwen, "Opposite Sexes or Neighboring Sexes?" in *Women, Ministry and the Gospel: Exploring New Paradigms,* Mark Husbands and Timothy Larsen, eds. (Downers Grove: InterVarsity, 2007), 173.

4. Van Leeuwen, "Opposite Sexes or Neighboring Sexes?" 174.

Chapter Five

Marriage as a Holy Union

Where Partnership is Most Intimate

The evening started as a date night. Jack and I had been married for just over a year. The combination of his graduate studies and part-time youth ministry and my full-time teaching job meant we had few evenings to spend relaxing together. We weren't so concerned about what movie we watched, we just wanted to get away.

Soon after the movie started, I knew we had made a mistake. It was an action thriller with graphic fire and explosions. Tears began to run down my face. I tried to quietly deal with them, but soon Jack noticed and asked if we needed to leave. We did. Sitting out in the car, I still could not gain my composure. Jack held me and let me cry it out. I felt so guilty that our date night was ruined and felt sure that somehow my grief was inappropriate at this time in my life.

I was crying about the death of my first husband, Mike Warren. He was killed in an explosion our senior year in college while helping volunteer fire fighters put out a grass fire near our country home.

Although I received a great deal of love, comfort, and support through Mike's death, I never seemed able to get past the sadness of it all. The advice of many older women who had experienced a similar loss was, "Grieve, grieve hard, and then get over it."

Jack and I met in the middle of my grief and formed a close relationship that eventually led to our marriage. That night as my tears continued, I looked up to see Jack crying as well. I apologized, saying that I knew I shouldn't still be grieving, but somehow I couldn't get over the tragedy of Mike's death.

"Is that what you think?" Jack asked me. "You think I'm upset because you're crying over Mike's death?"

I nodded.

"Jeanene," he said, "Don't you know that I love Mike too? He was part of you, he shaped the person you are and that I love. Mike is part of our lives and always will be. You don't ever have to be concerned about expressing your grief with me."

What could I say to that expression of mature love? I wasn't crying because I wanted Mike to still be my husband; I wouldn't have called him back from being with the Lord even if I could. And I loved Jack, deeply and profoundly, and was delighted to be spending the rest of my life with him. That night, however, something shifted for me. I had already felt loved, comforted, and secure with Jack. But now I found a place of belonging, of intimacy, and of great joy.

This discussion on partnership would not be complete without a chapter on marriage. Although I have been married most of my adult life and have spoken on the topic frequently, I am hesitant to write about it for many reasons. Marriage is the most intimate relationship that many of us experience and has the potential to bless or hurt us. Some couples, like Jack and I, live with a great deal of scrutiny of our marriages because of our positions within our community. We are often judged or criticized for how others see our marriage functioning.

Others have been deeply hurt by marriage through abuse, death, or divorce—whether it be our parents' or our own. Still others suffer grief over the fact that they never married and feel like second-class citizens, especially in the church. And too often, we portray marriage as the only appropriate, God-sanctioned partnership between men and women. As Christians, we are often not sensitive to these many reactions on the topic of marriage.

Thoughts on Working Together

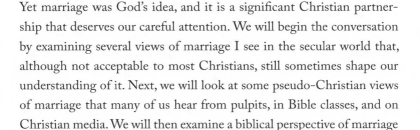

"From the very beginning, Christians [must] realize that our responsibilities do not include being an individual in the church. God calls us through Scripture to be part of the body, which is the whole of Christianity. With this dependence on others the obvious conclusion is working together. Thus comes the team. Ecclesiastes tells us that two are better than one because when two lay down they can keep warm. Being different creatures, the product is sometimes joy and others heartache."

—Male Student

Yet marriage was God's idea, and it is a significant Christian partnership that deserves our careful attention. We will begin the conversation by examining several views of marriage I see in the secular world that, although not acceptable to most Christians, still sometimes shape our understanding of it. Next, we will look at some pseudo-Christian views of marriage that many of us hear from pulpits, in Bible classes, and on Christian media. We will then examine a biblical perspective of marriage that has the potential to bless our marriages and focus them according to God's design. I hope that the material in this chapter will also bless our understanding of all partnerships and cause us to think how we function within them.

Secular Views of Marriage

I don't need a piece of paper. This view promotes the goodness of cohabitation outside the confines of marriage. Individuals in these relationships often say they stay because of love and commitment since they are not bound by any legality. They are free to move in and out of relationships unencumbered. When things get too difficult they can leave supposedly with less hassle and hurt than in a divorce. These types of break-ups are certainly less expensive for all involved. Others who hold this view may stay together for extended periods of time, even years. They often find a sense of stability and well-being; many report that they do not see the benefits of marriage. In some states, but not all, their union is considered a common-law marriage. While most Christians would find this view of relationship between men and women unpalatable, it is not without influence among us. I see too many people "living together" without marriage and feeling justified in doing so. Let me share a couple of experiences that I have had repeatedly.

Jake and Sara,[1] both Christians, came to me for premarital counseling. In the course of our discussion, they revealed that they were already "married in their hearts." When asked what this meant, they explained that they had already shared vows with each other and were sexually involved. They were only going through the formality of a wedding for their parents' sakes. As we discussed how they came to this understanding, it was clear that both felt they needed sex to find out if they were truly compatible, and they obviously were. However, as the counseling continued, they discovered other areas of major concern. Eventually, they broke off the engagement and went their separate ways.

In another case, Ashley came into my office crying because she could no longer deal with her roommate situation. Although she had signed a one-year lease, she was not sure that she could continue to live in the house with the present situation. As she talked, it came out that two of her roommates were having regular sleepovers with their boyfriends. When Ashley confronted them with the inappropriateness of their actions, they assured her that everything was fine. They explained to her that they were not literally having sex. They were retaining what many call "technical virginity" by participating in all forms of sexual expression except actual intercourse. When I called all the girls in for a conversation about their choices and the impact on those concerned, the roommates were surprised to discover that I thought what they were doing was not in keeping with a Christian commitment.

What's in it for me? People who hold this position seek relationship for the perceived benefit it holds for them. They may marry because their prospective spouse is especially attractive or wealthy. The marriage may offer financial security, social status, or the promise of emotional support. Marriage from this vantage point offers the elusive happiness sought by so many in our culture. Individuals who hold this view often have selfish impulses and unreasonable expectations of what it takes to make a marriage work. Again, we may be tempted to assume that Christians would not be easily influenced by such shallow impulses, but experience tells me otherwise.

Andy and Susan were fellow graduate students with us. They were one of the few couples we knew at that time who were practicing Christians. Andy pursued his doctorate during the day while Susan watched the children. She worked the night shift as a nurse so that they didn't have to pay for childcare. Both of them were exhausted much of the time, but Susan seemed barely able to function at times from lack of sleep. Somehow, they felt it was all worth it to pursue their dreams and nurture their children. Imagine our surprise when, right after graduation, Andy announced that he was leaving Susan for another woman. He reported that Susan was no longer his intellectual equal but his new girlfriend definitely was. He suggested that perhaps his and Susan's marriage had been best for getting him through grad school but was not meant to be a lifetime partnership.

Another time, we sat in our living room talking with close friends. Celia had told us the week before that she had simply outgrown their marriage. She wanted time to travel, to have some adventures, to be free from the responsibilities of job, husband, and children. When we asked if she couldn't pursue those interests without abandoning her family, she said, "No. For once I have to think about what's best for me. I've spent most of my life putting others first, but now it's my time." As she walked out, she gave us a line that I have heard too many times from people who ought to know better: "I just know that God wants me to be happy." I didn't know what to say in response. Should I suggest that God wants her to be unhappy? We sat there for a few more minutes trying to absorb what had just happened. I have often wondered if Celia found the happiness she so desired, and if it was enough. We will talk more about the pursuit of happiness later in the chapter.

Few Christians would embrace either of these views of marriage. Yet they creep into our subconsciouses and affect the ways in which we see our marriages and ourselves. It is not surprising that as they do, we seek ways to justify the resulting negative thoughts and actions by appealing to God. What we end up with are distorted pictures of humanity, of relationships, and of the Divine. I would suggest that equally damaging are pseudo-Christian views of marriage. While they may seem to be more spiritual at first glance, they too lead us away from God's intention for how we are to be in our most intimate relationships.

Pseudo-Christian Views of Marriage

The family that prays together, stays together. I have seen this phrase on billboards in numerous cities and on more church marquees than I care to count. I am confident that anyone reading this chapter will wonder what is the matter with this truism? Isn't prayer important for believing Christians? How can this possibly not be a good motto for Christian men and women striving to keep God at the center of their home and relationship? I understand the concern. But what I find to be most problematic is how the phrase begins. The focus is on the human relationships and how God can make them stick if we simply engage in spiritual practices. I'm not questioning the priority of prayer but rather its place in this schema.

We often talk about the problem of idolatry in biblical times. When we discuss what possible idols exist today, we list things such as cars, homes, paychecks, vacations, etc. What I find troubling, however, is that for many Christians our marriages, and subsequently our families, are our idols. They misplace God and become the center of our lives. And in the process, the church is reduced to being just another resource to be used by the family. I am not saying that we shouldn't value our families and allow the church to help us with them, but I think the question of what is central is a critical one. And that leads to a second view, which has the same underlying problem as this one but with a different center of focus.

As long as we are focused on Christian service, our marriage will be fine. While I have never heard this view spoken aloud, I have certainly witnessed it being lived out. I am not exactly sure of its root, but I can think of several possibilities. Perhaps it grows out of a works-righteousness understanding of salvation—the belief that we have to earn our way to heaven. Or maybe it is a way to bargain with God—I'll serve you in this way Lord so that you will (fill in the blank). Or it may be a way to get attention—accolades from all kinds of people about my good works. Possibly it is linked to compulsive behavior that has been put to good use—at least other people are being helped. Or it may be a cover for low self esteem and intimacy issues that have never been dealt with—busyness for the

Lord at least offers some release. Whatever the source, this approach to relationship also misplaces God and potentially damages relationships.

Ministry to others is part of any committed Christian life. But if it misplaces God's rightful place as the center of our lives, then it too becomes a form of idolatry, and even worse. I think that for many over-committed servants, their ministry becomes their love affair. They are practicing a form of spiritual adultery that has all of the same ramifications of relational adultery. And yet, who can question them about it? After all, they are only doing the Lord's work.

Thoughts on Working Together

"I learned many important principles about working in a group setting. First of all, I must be willing to take a back seat. I cannot always be the one to lead every project and solve every problem. This was a hard lesson for me to learn because I like being in charge and carrying the weight of the decisions. Throughout this project, however, I had to take a back seat because my time was divided between this project and my daughter. I was forced to share responsibility because I knew that I would not be successful if I took on many heavy responsibilities. I also learned that my team members eagerly carried their weight and had no problem dispersing responsibilities evenly."

—Female Student

The offended spouse in this relationship is in a catch-22—nothing he or she can say or do seems to be able to get to the real source of the problem. Just as in physical affairs the offending spouse is able to project the difficulties back onto his or her offended mate. Think of the possibilities:

1) obviously the accusing spouses don't love the Lord as much, 2) perhaps they misunderstand the importance of a particular ministry, 3) possibly they are underestimating the offenders' significant contributions to ministry, or 4) maybe they just need to learn to be more supportive.

What troubles me about both of these views is not only their prevalence, but also how destructive they can be. I am confident that there are other such pseudo-Christian views of marriage but these two at least put us on the alert and prepare us to consider what I believe is God's intention for our marriages.

God's Design for Marriage

Covenant. The word conjures up all kinds of responses. For some, it refers to a binding contract in which each person signing must be careful to read the fine print. For others, it may be an amiable agreement that both enter hoping for the best. For Christians, however, covenant is tied to the nature of God. Throughout the Hebrew Bible, we read of God, who is holy and faithful, entering a covenant with human beings who are flawed and sinful. Familial language describes God's tender love for the people (see Hosea 11:3–4, Isa. 66:13) and none is more intimate than in the use of the marriage metaphor (Hosea 2:16, 19–20). The prophet Isaiah records this message from God to Israel: "Do not fear, for I have redeemed you; I have called you by name, you are mine. . . . Because you are precious in my sight, and honored, and I love you" (Isa. 43:1a, 4a).

It is not surprising that Christians have adopted this loving, intimate expectation of covenant as a lens through which we see the sacred union of marriage. For Christians, this connection means that the covenant of marriage is not only made between the husband and wife but also with God. Also, the covenant is considered valid only after others witness it, a practice still required to complete most marriage licenses. The ceremony binding the covenant, the wedding, includes witnesses but also is full of the promises of fulfillment. Just as God promises faithfulness, steadfast-ness, and constancy to Israel, so the man and woman commit to live with God and one another.

Traditional marriage vows mirror all of these expectations: "I, _____, take you _____, to be my [wife/husband], to have and to hold, for better or for worse, for richer, for poorer, in sickness and in health, to love and to cherish; from this day forward until death do us part." With these promises, death is the only thing that can sever the marriage relationship. "I'll stay with you," the couples declare, "no matter what."

One-flesh. The first chapter of Genesis ends with God blessing the newly created man and woman and giving them the cultural mandate to "be fruitful and multiply, and fill the earth and subdue it; and have dominion [over all creation]" (Gen. 1:28ff). At the end of chapter two, God's direc-tive is different: "Therefore a man leaves his father and his mother and clings to his wife, and they become one flesh. And the man and his wife were both naked, and were not ashamed" (Gen. 2:24–25). Both passages clearly refer to sexual union, even though neither states it explicitly. Yet the process of becoming one flesh is far greater than the joining of the male and female bodies physically in marriage. I would suggest that God is creating a whole new being—a marriage. I have heard it described in mathematical terms: one whole person plus one other whole person in marriage does not equal two but one. The man and the woman bring all that they are to this union but lose none of the fullness of who each is as a person in doing so. Any other construct means that a woman is only a half without a man and vice versa—a perspective that was articulated in the movie *Jerry Maguire.* When the leading male, Tom Cruise, finally comes to his senses and realizes that he loves the leading female, Rene Zellwegger, he tells her, "You complete me." Without her, would he be less of a human being? So many of us imply the same sentiment when we speak about marriage. (And we wonder why the singles among us feel second-rate?) The best way I can illustrate this idea is through the lens of my own marriage.

Several years ago our family "adopted" one of our international students, Sunny, from South Korea. She is a delightful young woman who enriched our lives immeasurably. When she first arrived in the States, she struggled not only to converse in English but also to understand cultural expectations. If you know anything about most Asian cultures, showing honor to those who are older is a strong social value. Jack and I, however, were in a unique relationship with Sunny. She was both our daughter and our student. She did not know what to call us. Mom and Dad was too intimate, Jack and Jeanene too casual, and so she addressed us as Dr. Janeese (a combination of Jack, Jeanene, and Reese). We loved it. Unwittingly, she gave "us" a singular name.

Jack and I have been married a number of years. This year, he is 59 years old and I am 58. Our marriage, however, is not the sum of the two of us in terms of age or maturity. If it were, it would be 117 years old! Rather our marriage is a 35-year-old relationship. It is a young adult in that sense and must be treated as such. Just think of the difference it would make if we allowed our marriages to be treated as one-year-olds, ten-year-olds, twenty-year-olds, and so on. Wouldn't our expectations be different? Our approach to its care and nurturing altered?

Our unity in marriage reflects the unity of the Trinity, and the joining of the male and female, both made in the image of God, allows marriage to reflect God's glory and God's nature. The one-flesh perspective also upholds Jesus' teaching on marriage found in the Gospels (Mark 10:2–12; Matt. 19:3–12). In both accounts, the Pharisees question Jesus about the legality of divorce and note that Moses allowed husbands to give their wives a certificate of divorce. Jesus answered their first question by referencing Genesis 2:24, "'For this reason a man shall leave his father and mother and be joined to his wife, and the two shall become one flesh.' So they are no longer two, but one flesh. Therefore what God has joined together, let no one separate" (Mark 10:6–9; Matt. 19:5–6).

In addressing the Pharisees, Jesus made it clear that God is the one who joins the man and woman. In English, the word "join" has the potential for a double meaning—God is the one who brings them together creating a marriage, and God becomes part of the marriage. Yet in Greek, the meaning is entirely different, join carries the sense of being yoked together.[2] And what do we yoke together and for what purpose? We yoke oxen for the purpose of work. Not a very romantic picture but a very realistic one.

Work is intrinsic to the relationship of marriage. We establish homes, bear children, work jobs, and hopefully contribute to the good of the community. For Christians, however, the work is even more significant. Our marriages are formed for work in God's Kingdom. I have often wished that at weddings we asked, "Do we have the yoke ready?" instead of "Do we have rings?" It would certainly be a more sobering moment for all concerned. Though not exactly the same, I did once hear a question asked with a similar sentiment in mind.

We all watched with delight as two of my closest friends growing up, Mark and Karen,[3] started dating, fell in love, and decided to be married. She was the maid of honor at my first wedding and both were attendants for Jack and me. I was the matron of honor at their wedding, and Mark's grandfather, a very godly man, performed the ceremony. At the place where the traditional question is asked, "Does anyone have a just cause why this man and woman should not be married?" he asked something far more significant. He addressed the audience and asked, "Does anyone know why the wedding of these two, Karen and Mark, will hinder either of them from being with the Lord when he comes again?" What a great question! I will tell you that I do not know of any marriage that has served the church more faithfully than theirs.

This yoke perspective is also useful in answering many of the questions that surround the decision about whom to marry or whether to marry or not. If we used godly principles to make these decisions, then our marriages would be more likely to fit God's purposes. In situations where people are not sure if they should marry some particular person, I advise them to consider what living with that person will mean for their lifetime commitments to Christ. If the romantic relationship will hinder the spiritual, the individual inquiries have an answer.

When Jack and I met, we both had come to the conclusion that we would serve God as singles. I was recently widowed, and he saw no apparent prospects for marriage. We were both headed toward different ministries and were prepared to be unmarried. When it became obvious, however, that our relationship had the potential to be a serious one, we asked ourselves: Would we be more effective serving together or alone? The conclusion we came to seems obvious now, but it was not made without a lot of prayer and wise counsel.

Looking back at Jesus' conversation with the Pharisees, we see that there is more to the discussion. The second part of their inquiry focuses on the fact that Moses permitted certificates of divorce to be written. Jesus explained that this action was allowed only because of the hardness of the people's hearts. Divorce was never part of God's plan. We know that God hates divorce (Mal. 2:16).

In both Gospel accounts, Jesus has even more to say. According to Matthew, the only acceptable reason for divorce is sexual infidelity; in Mark, Jesus says that anyone who marries a divorced person commits adultery. These teachings have been the source of much debate among Christians. It is not my intention to undertake a full treatment of divorce and remarriage in this discussion. However, I think we must consider a few elements.

I want to acknowledge first how difficult it is to discuss divorce because of its potential to hurt many people—those who have chosen it and those who have suffered from others' choices. I have both family members and dear friends who have suffered the trauma and pain of divorce. I do not know one of them who would say that is an easy or good choice at all. Yet circumstances sometimes leave people in impossible situations.

At the same time, as Christians, we have so emphasized what we often call "scriptural grounds" for divorce that I think some people resort to adultery as a means of getting out of a bad marriage. Too often we begin our marriages with a tiny clause in the covenant. I'll stay with you unless one of us commits adultery. Knowing Jesus' desire for marriage to be for a lifetime, I am confident that he did not intend for us to enter it with a loophole. It seems as if we think it is easier to be forgiven for adultery than for divorce. Divorce is not an unforgiveable sin. I believe the church can hold up the sanctity of marriage and still journey with those whose marriages have failed. I am committed to both.

The concept of covenant is a good lens through which we see marriage, but the metaphor of one-flesh best represents God's design for it. The author of Ephesians, in discussing how Christian wives and husbands should relate to one another, also refers to Genesis 2:24 but applies it to Christ and the church. It is one of three mysteries revealed in the epistle. The first is that God reconciled humanity to God's self (1:7b–10). The second is that God reconciled Jews and Gentiles to one another and made them joint heirs of the Kingdom (3:1–6). The third is that Christ is the loving head over his bride, the church (5:31–32). Since the final mystery is revealed in the context of headship and submission for husbands and wives, it seems only appropriate to examine it next.

Headship and Submission

Several years ago, I was involved in several evangelistic studies. One young woman, Sandra, was so eager to hear about Jesus that she actually knocked on my door and asked me to study with her. Of course, I was delighted and soon she committed her life to Christ and was baptized.

Her husband, Tony, supported her faith decision but was not very interested in following suit. Sandra was convinced that if he studied with us he would eventually become a Christian.

Jack and I agreed to meet with them and talk about how to have a better marriage. Sandra thought that this approach might be easier for Tony to take than a more direct one. At our first meeting, Tony suggested that if we would just tell Sandra what the Bible said about wives obeying their husbands, there would be no need for further discussion. Even though Tony had limited knowledge of Scripture, he knew Ephesians 5:22, or at least he thought he did.

In that moment, Tony made the same mistake that many of us make in approaching Scripture—he pulled something completely out of its context, made it say what he wanted to hear, and applied it to his immediate situation. But the text he used, just like all Scripture, has a specific context that must be considered if we are to better understand its meaning. Insights on how the church at Ephesus was established and some of the developments that took place within it are found in various places in the New Testament other than Ephesians (see Acts 18:24–20:1, 17–38; 1 and 2 Tim.; Rev. 2:1–7). It is obvious when reading these that the Ephesian church struggled with issues of spiritual power, false teaching, and faithful leadership.

In writing to the church, Paul focuses the first three chapters on who God is and what God has done on behalf of all Christians.[4] This section of the letter lays the theological foundation from which the rest of the book flows. It ends with Paul's powerful prayer for the believers to know all the fullness of God (3:19). In the last three chapters, Paul focuses on how believers ought to live, beginning with the words, "I therefore, the prisoner of the Lord, beg you to lead a life worthy of the calling to which you have been called, with all humility and gentleness, with patience, bearing with one another in love, making every effort to maintain the unity of the Spirit in the bond of peace" (4:1–3).

Interwoven throughout the instruction found in chapters 4–6 are further theological insights that keep Christian conduct tied to God's nature and activity. Look for example at Ephesians 4:17–24. In this section, Christians are told to abandon their former way of life and to put on the new self "according to the likeness of God in true righteousness and holiness" (24). The same is true of the second half of Ephesians 5, the section from which Tony took his misunderstanding of marital relations. Here Christians are given a series of injunctions that organize the ideas. We are to "be careful how [we] live not as unwise people but as wise" (5:15); "be filled with the Spirit" as we address one another (5:18b); and "be subject to one another out of reverence for Christ" (5:21). Each of these represents a basic tenet of life in Christ: a faithful life filled with wisdom, a Spirit-filled countenance that encourages others, and a submissive posture that flows from our reverence for the Lord.

Immediately following these instructions we find a household code, a societal structure usually addressed to the ruler of the household, the *paterfamilias*, who held absolute power over his subjects (wives, children, and slaves).[5] However, several elements of this household code are substantially different from those found in extra-biblical codes. Not least is the fact that these instructions are placed within what Richard B. Hays calls "a vision for community whose social relations are impacted by the gospel of Jesus Christ."[6]

The hierarchical structure of the code is tempered by the comprehensive nature of the call to the whole church to live with the basic tenets of Christian faith listed above. The structure of this particular code is also quite distinct: Most ancient codes were addressed only to the person who held power. In turn, that individual was given instruction for his subordinates. In Paul's structure, the subordinates are addressed and are called to *choose* a submissive position, something unheard of in the ancient world. Paul's code in Ephesians 5 is also reciprocal—the least powerful in the house is called to submit to the most powerful, but the one in the ruling position is challenged to act in a Christ-like manner, with humility and gentleness (6:5–9). It is hard for us today to imagine the impact these kinds of changes would have had on those receiving Paul's letter.

We may be tempted to ask, why did the apostle not abolish the injustices found in the extreme subordination of women, children, and slaves? But any overt challenge to Rome's power would have been immediately squelched. Instead, Paul is demonstrating a unique example of cultural engagement. Rather than overturning the conventional authority structure, Paul chooses to subvert it.[7] In so doing, he allows the household code not only to serve those in the community according to Christ's lordship and example but also to be a witness to the rest of the world.

I don't think we have any unified household codes in the U.S. today. That is not to say that we can't take the principles Paul is giving in this letter and apply them to our relationships. Of course we can. But instead of spending so much time defining headship and what it means for husbands or discovering how submission must be practiced by wives, what if we gospeled our one-flesh partnerships, putting them under the lordship of Jesus Christ? The results would not only bless those relationships but also serve as a witness to those outside of Christ. We would once again engage our culture through transformed lives in surprising and effective ways.

Back to Tony's comment about Sandra "obeying" him. That night, Jack and I did not have all of the insights that have come in later years of life together and study of God's word. What we *were* able to tell him was that the word for obedience is not applied in Scripture to the marriage relationship except once. In 1 Corinthians 7:3–5, Paul instructs believers on how to conduct themselves sexually within the marriage. He explains that the wife has authority over her husband's body and he over hers. It is a mutually expressive and fulfilling relationship.

Instead of writing this chapter as a guide to marriage, I have tried to take us behind this partnership to see what God intended it to be. In these last paragraphs, I would like to explore a premise that came to me through one of my favorite books on marriage, *Sacred Marriage: What if God Designed Marriage to Make Us Holy More Than to Make Us Happy?*[8] I am indebted to author Gary Thomas for many of the insights that follow.

Holy vs. Happy

When I ask almost any group of parents what they really want for their children, many share the same response. "All I want," they say, "is for my children to be happy." I am floored every time I hear it. Let me assure you that I am not trying to make my children unhappy. I just don't think happiness is the goal. Yet many of us chase this illusive emotion and never quite catch it. I think it is why we accumulate so many things, why we strive for bigger, better positions, why we anesthetize our children with entertainment, and why we become convinced that our spouses just aren't cutting it.

Happiness has the same root as "happenings." Often, what we are seeking is just the right set of circumstances so that we can be happy. But circumstances rarely work out like we want—and frankly, I don't think God cares that much about our happiness. What God desires is for us to be changed more and more into the likeness of Jesus Christ. Marriage becomes a crucible, an intense way for God to teach us, through great joy and deep sorrow, exactly what that means. I would like to give attention to three of the principles Thomas examines in his book.

Marriage teaches us to love like God loves. Anytime we practice love, we can assume that God is at work whether we acknowledge it or not. For we know "... love is from God; everyone who loves is born of God and knows God. Whoever does not love does not know God, for God is love" (1 John 4:7b–8). And marriage is all about love, or at least it's supposed to be.

Many of us remember the beautiful days of first love. When everything the other said was funny or insightful. When I found my spouse's idiosyncrasies intriguing and his faults endearing. When we thought each other so appealing that we could hardly keep our hands off each other.

But it doesn't last long and it shouldn't. To live in that sort of dream world is not to experience real life, or I would suggest, real love. After all, we are yoked for a purpose.

Soon the daily grind of bills, jobs, housework, children, yards, mortgages, cars, repairs, and more takes a toll. If we are not attentive, we soon slip into a myriad of bad habits that eat away at the joy of the relationship and erode the love we share. But if we keep God at the center, things can be different. I remember vividly watching an older, well-respected couple greet one another with warmth and enthusiasm after only being separated from each other for a matter of hours. I asked the wife, Freda, how they kept that "spark" alive. I expected her to give me some insight that I could file away to use in the future. Instead she said, "The Lord is right there in the middle of us." I wanted to say, "I knew that." But I didn't really. Instead of giving me something I could store for the future, she gave me the key to living every day as a Christian wife.

Do I always feel love? No. Love is not an emotional response but an ongoing choice. There are times, however, when I don't even have the will to choose love. Jack and I, like all married couples, have experienced our share of hard times. I used to think that if things got difficult enough that I couldn't love with my love, I could always love with God's. Then I discovered that I cannot love with God's love unless I am fully surrendered to it.

The choice to keep God at the center of my marriage begins with the choice to keep God at the center of my life. Only when I choose to be a loving, committed person am I able to also be that kind of spouse. And this decision is a daily one. It does not occur automatically across the span of my life or my marriage. Just as God is continually transforming me, so God is at work in us to make our partnership what it needs to be.

Marriage teaches us to be faithful as God is faithful. It is interesting that God uses the marriage union as an analogy for God's relationship with

Israel. The whole book of Hosea is about the prophet's faithfulness in marriage to his adulterous wife, Gomer. Their human relationship mirrors the spiritual union between Israel and God. Yet this analogy or metaphor is not what most of us have in mind when we think of our marriage. We prefer the loving, sacrificial metaphor discussed earlier from Ephesians 5. There, Christ, the bridegroom, sacrifices everything in order to present the church, his bride, in splendor and glory.

In a recent television interview, Elizabeth Edwards, wife of John Edwards, spoke about his sexual affair and the subsequent book she wrote about their lives. He was one of the last three candidates for the Democratic nominee for president. During the campaign, doctors discovered that Elizabeth had cancer, but the Edwards decided to proceed with the grueling schedule anyway. John eventually withdrew from the election process when it became apparent he would not win the nomination.

Months later, John Edwards' affair became public and the news broke that he fathered the other woman's child. In spite of it all, the Edwards tried to keep their lives together. One comment that Elizabeth made during the telecast, however, really stuck with me. She said, "All I ever asked of John was that he be faithful to me." She, of course, meant that she never wanted him to betray her with another woman. And now he had.

I bring this situation up with hesitancy. I do not want to be guilty of undermining the gravity of their situation or of removing the expectation for sexual faithfulness in marriage. And of course, none of us can know what goes on in any marriage behind closed doors. But in our celebrity-obsessed, media-driven culture, short sound bytes often take on the weight of truth. While I can't make any assertions about John and Elizabeth Edwards' marriage, I have watched adultery impact the live of couples I love dearly. What I do want to challenge, however, is the sense that faithfulness means never faltering. None of us are able to walk in perfection in any of our relationships. We are all sinners.

We hurt one another and betray one another in small and large ways. And each time we do, we are given another opportunity to repent and to forgive. I cannot imagine what marriage would be like without both of these elements.

Marriage teaches us to bear witness to God's activity in our lives. Sometimes we get so caught up in the daily pressures that we fail to stop and take stock of what God is actually doing in our lives. Years ago, Jack and I began a practice that has really blessed our marriage. We have a five-year review. I would love to say that we thought through this process carefully and initiated it intentionally, but in truth, we stumbled into it. At our fifth anniversary, we were just beginning to realize some of our life goals. As we talked about them, we looked back over our time together and realized how gracious the Lord had been to us in the good and bad times.

At ten years of marriage, we did the same. This time, I was very pregnant with our third child, Jack was busy preaching to a growing church, and our conversation was quite different. By now, however, we had established a pattern of looking for how God was blessing us and challenging us in our life together. I highly recommend the practice and look forward to our next anniversary—our thirty-fifth. Who knows what God will accomplish by then?

What I think is most encouraging is not only the opportunity to acknowledge God's activity in our lives but to share it with others. In the movie, *Shall We Dance?* the female lead says, "We all want a witness to our lives." She is sharing it in the context of why we want to be married. I agree with her in part. I think all of us want to think that our lives, our marriages, our children, our heritage matter. But for Christians none of those are actually our own; they belong to God. When we share not only this reality but also how God is at work in all of them, then we are witnesses for the gospel in our time and in our place.

So who benefits from living with the expectation that marriage is designed to make us holy instead of happy? I think the first blessing goes to the husband and wife. Living with an open heart to what God will teach us in our marriages brings a sense of deep joy and peace instead of disappointment and failure. We know that it is not all up to us, we have help from the Lord and from the community of faith. Also, our children witness the authenticity with which we relate to one another and to them. They gain a greater sense of security and hope for how their lives can be in the Lord and in their future relationships, married or otherwise.

Thoughts on Working Together

"I learned that being in teams when I get into full time ministry can be a great benefit to me but also a great task. It is not as simple as it seems, and lots of feelings can get hurt when working together. I have learned that I need to become more flexible, encouraging, loving, and patient before I am ready to go into partnership in ministry. I can also see the importance of communicating honestly with one another because I am just now realizing that a lot of the things that I wrote down I never discussed with my teammates. Doing so could have lightened a lot of the stress and frustration that I am realizing now that I have."

—Male Student

Our church and our neighbors also are blessed when we live in pursuit of holiness and not happiness. I am always aware that others are watching us. Yes, some watch out of simple curiosity—we are a weird bunch. Others observe in order to criticize—vultures are often on the horizon. But still others want to learn how to be in marriage, how to raise children, and how to do it all in the Lord. Our homes can become a refuge to people as our lives are beacons of light. Our being vulnerable and needing help does not diminish our witness. Actually, I believe it offers others hope. No one I know is looking for people who have their act together. Most people want to know that God will bless even our messes.

Conclusion

Looking back to that night after the movie, I am astonished at the sweetness and wisdom we shared that night. The thirty-five years Jack and I have had together have been rich. Many of them filled with a sense of purpose, closeness, excitement, and fulfillment. Others have been difficult, challenging, and full of disappointment. Yet I wouldn't change one of them.

We have learned a lot about what it means to really partner together. We have raised three children, seen two of them marry wonderful partners, and now have two beautiful grandchildren and the hope of more in the future.

God has blessed each of us with rich ministry opportunities. But we recognize that our family is just one small link in a long line of faithful men and women, married and single, who have lived holy lives.

There is a beautiful song that we have sung in worship and for weddings. The words always resonate in my heart and tonight, as I close this chapter, the tune has been playing constantly in my head.

Will all who come behind us find us faithful?
Will the fire of our devotion light their way?
Will the footprints that we leave,
Lead them to believe
And the lives we live inspire them to obey?
Oh will all who come behind us find us faithful?[9]

I hope the answer is yes, Lord. Please make it so.

Notes to Chapter Five

1. Names of all individuals mentioned in this chapter have been changed to protect their real identity, unless otherwise specified.

2. The word in Greek is "suzeugnumi" (from the combination of "zeugnumi," meaning "to yoke," and "sun," meaning "with" or "together," so that the word takes on the meaning of "to yoke together, join, or unite"). The same word is used in both Mark 10:9 and Matthew 19:6. It is also found in 2 Corinthian 6:14 when Paul instructs Christians not to be "misyoked" with unbelievers. *The Analytical Greek Lexicon Revised,* edited by Harold K. Moulton (Grand Rapids: Zondervan, 1977), 380.

3. These names are real. Mark and Karen Howell serve the Sugar Grove Church of Christ in Houston, Texas. He is the preacher and she works in various ministries. They are widely known for their faithfulness and love toward each other and many in their community.

4. Many contemporary scholars do not think that the apostle Paul is the author of Ephesians. The tradition of the church, however, is that Paul did write it, and for convenience in this discussion, I will proceed with the latter understanding.

5. Household codes are also found in Colossians 3:18–4:1, Titus 2:1–10, and 1 Peter 2:18–3:7. For a brief but excellent treatment of the context of Roman culture and household codes, see Michael Kruse, "Theology and Economics: Paul's Subversion of the Empire," March 16, 2006, http://krusekronicle.typepad.com/kruse_kronicle/2006/03/theology_and_ec_5.html.

6. Richard B. Hays, *The Moral Vision of the New Testament: Contemporary Introduction to New Testament Ethics* (Edinburgh: T & T Clark, 1997), 64–65.

7. Ibid., 64.

8. Gary Thomas, *Sacred Marriage: What if God Designed Marriage to Make Us Holy More Than to Make Us Happy?* (Grand Rapids: Zondervan, 2000). I cannot tell you how much I love Gary's work. We have given this book to all of our adult children and to many of our children in the faith. I highly recommend it.

9. Jon Mohr, "Find Us Faithful," Birdwing Music/Jonathan Mark Music (admin. by the Sparrow Corp. in Brentwood, Tennessee), 1988.

Chapter Six

A Christian Response to It All

What God Desires from Us

The house was very quiet and the children still asleep when I slipped into the living room to finish my preparation for teaching a midweek Bible class. We were studying the gospels, and I was to teach the parable of the unmerciful servant (Matt. 18:21–35).

It was a hectic time in our lives, with busy ministries, community involvement, and children's activities. I rarely had a minute to sit down, much less spend meaningful time in study and prayer. That morning as I looked over my notes, the opening question I had prepared really struck me: Have you ever had a situation in which you found it especially difficult to forgive?

Hurling from my past came an instance in my own life when I failed to forgive someone who had once been close to me. I knew that I could not teach this lesson without asking God to help me forgive others in my own past.

As I prayed, I was dismayed at the number of hurts that I had accumulated over the years. Even worse was the realization that I often shared with others situations from the now-distant relationship that offended me, and I enjoyed watching their sympathetic reactions. These moments

147

justified my lack of forgiveness and allowed me to hold the related hurt even closer. Soon my prayer shifted from asking God to help me forgive my former friend and partner to asking God to forgive me for my lack of forgiveness.

When I arrived at the church building that morning, I laid aside the lesson I had prepared. I knew that there was no way to begin the class but by confessing my sin and calling others to do the same. For the next hour and a half, Christians gathered in small clusters to share their hearts with one another. They sought and gave forgiveness as they prayed for one another. It was one of the most powerful sessions we shared during that series.

What began then and continues today is a journey in forgiveness. I want to begin this chapter by acknowledging that I have grown through this experience and others like it, but I remain a work in progress. Sometimes I wish I had a sign around my neck alerting everyone to this important fact. I have been blessed to see forgiveness being given and received by significant individuals in my life. I have also faced situations with family, friends, and fellow Christians that I thought I would never have to deal with, and yet I've found myself having to offer forgiveness and asking to be forgiven. God has taught me much along the way, but I am confident I still have much more to learn.

Partnerships do fail. Sometimes we are the offenders, sometimes the offended. The situations that cause us difficulty vary from small slights and insensitivities to larger betrayals and deep divisions. Whatever the circumstances, each time there is failure, partners have new opportunities to consider how we will respond and what will happen to the relationships involved. In this final chapter, I would like to explore the critical place that forgiveness plays in how we live and work together.

Two main realities about forgiveness will focus this discussion. We will look first at how forgiveness is a great gift we have been given, and then we will consider how forgiveness is an equally great gift that we give to others. In the final section of the chapter, we will turn our attention to how we can make forgiveness a way of life. I am confident that in the process of writing these things, I will discover even greater areas of need in my partnerships for forgiveness; I pray that readers do the same.

Thoughts on Working Together

"Respect was an unspoken partner with us during our project. We shared open and honest dialogue. Listening to each other's ideas about how to best accomplish the task at hand allowed us to brainstorm and often led to a meshing of ideas. I felt no hesitation in making suggestions to my team members, and I felt no disappointment if my idea wasn't put to use. We were like family, and all worked together for the common good."

—Female Student

Forgiveness as a Gift We Have Received

Several years ago, I returned to see a therapist who previously had helped me deal with issues from my past. At our first meeting, he asked me why I seemed so upset at the idea of coming back to see him. I told him, "I have already dealt with all of this stuff." He then asked me a very profound question: "Jeanene," he said, "is your salvation a one-time event?" I responded that it wasn't. I acknowledged that salvation is past, I have been saved; it is present, I am being saved; and it is future, I will be saved. "The same is true of your healing," he responded. I have revisited this expression again and again in the years since. I also came to realize that it applies to forgiveness—in every instance where forgiveness is needed, it too is past, present, and future.

This reality, however, is not simply a therapeutic statement; it is also a theological truth. Throughout the Hebrew Bible, we repeatedly witness God's faithfulness in relationship to Israel's unfaithfulness. Moses appealed to God's loving, steadfast nature when Israel sinned repeatedly by not trusting God's provision for them. Moses used God's own words as a challenge to forgive the people again:

> And now, therefore, let the power of the Lord be great in the way that you promised when you spoke saying, "The Lord is slow to anger, and abounding in steadfast love, forgiving iniquity and transgression, but by no means clearing the guilty, visiting the iniquity of the parents upon the children to the third and fourth generation." Forgive the iniquity of this people according to the greatness of your steadfast love, just as you have pardoned this people, from Egypt even until now. (Num. 14:17–23)

We also hear stories of individuals sinning and God forgiving them. Just reading the story of David's adultery with Bathsheba and the resulting death of her husband is enough to help us see the great capacity God has to forgive our individual sins (2 Sam. 11:1–12:25). David cries out to God not only for forgiveness, but also for full restoration of their loving relationship (see Ps. 51). God honors David's request.

At this point we often want to say, "Well, we can be forgiven if we ask for it and show true repentance." And Jesus does connect repentance and forgiveness (Luke 17:1–4). Yet on the cross, Jesus modeled the gift of forgiveness to those who were both unrepentant and undeserving; they didn't even know they needed forgiveness. He implored God to forgive those who tormented and ultimately crucified him (Luke 23:34). Does this request minimize the need for repentance and confession? Clearly not. What I think it indicates, rather, is the great extent to which God will go to offer forgiveness to all. At our baptism, each of us is given not only the gift of the Holy Spirit, but also the forgiveness of our sins (Acts 2:38). As we continue to walk faithfully in the Lord, our sins are repeatedly forgiven and our lives made clean (1 John 1:5–10).

Yet sometimes forgiveness is a gift not well-received. When Jack and I first began dating, one of his good friends, Karen, said something that has stuck with me all these years. She said, "The greatest gift one can give a friend is to receive her gift well." I think she realized that I don't always receive gifts well. Rather, I am a neurotic giver. I assume it is my responsibility in almost every situation to be the one who gives and serves. Although it sounds like a lovely trait, and at times it is, it can also be terribly annoying, even hurtful. Ask my husband, my children, my closest friends. They will all tell you that I go to extremes with it and hinder their expressions of love. In being unable to receive a gift I am often selfish and willful even if my desire is to be selfless and submissive. When I rush to serve before anyone else has a chance, I inadvertently create obstacles that are difficult for others to overcome. In these instances I am, in essence, denying others the joy of giving when I cannot receive what they offer. And it is no different in our relationships with God.

I have counseled dozens of individuals who cannot seem to get over their sins (and therefore themselves). If we refuse to receive God's forgiveness we need to think of what we are saying to God: "Sorry, Lord, all the blood of Jesus is not enough to cover this situation; I need something more." Would we dare speak such a thing? Probably not. Yet I would suggest when we do not receive the gift of forgiveness from God and other Christians, we are basically making such a declaration. We fail to receive one of the most wonderful gifts ever given.

What does this have to do with our partnerships? I think everything. If I live in a state of constantly receiving God's gift of forgiveness, then

I become more fully aware of two vital understandings: I am a sinner in need of God's mercy and forgiveness, and I must honor God's gift of forgiveness by forgiving others as I am forgiven.

Forgiveness as a Gift We Must Give

Recognizing that forgiveness is tied to the nature of God, that it is given to us even when we do not deserve it, and that it was purchased with the sacrifice of Jesus' life—these seem like they would inspire us to be extremely forgiving of one another. Yet I find just the opposite to be true. Just as I confessed in the opening story, too many of us are guilty of holding on to our grudges and feeding them like we would a hungry child. Just as we delight in the growth and strength that child gains through nourishment, so we watch gleefully as our negative feelings get bigger and stronger. We justify our unwillingness to forgive and too often lose sight of the damage we're doing to others, to ourselves, and to the community of God. Our inability to forgive one another is one of the greatest obstacles we face in our partnerships.

I think Jesus knew that forgiveness would be especially challenging. In Matthew 18, he outlines how believers should handle situations in which one member of the church sins against another (18:15–20). They are first to go to the person in loving confrontation. If the problem continues, they are to take another person or two to discuss the matter with the offender. If there is still no resolution, the matter should be taken to the whole church. If the guilty individual is still unrepentant, he or she should be treated as an outcast. But even in sending someone away from the community, the goal is still, ultimately, restoration. These same principles guide our actions toward fellow sinners even today. But I also find it quite interesting what occurs just after this teaching.

Peter asks Jesus how many times he must forgive a fellow believer who has sinned against him. "As many as seven times?" Jesus responds, "Not seven times, but, I tell you, seventy-seven times" (18:21–22). Peter wants term limits and Jesus refuses to give them. Forgiveness is boundless for those who live in Christ. Jesus concludes by telling the parable of the unmerciful servant who was forgiven an impossible debt by his master and then refused to forgive a fellow slave who owed him only a pittance (18:23–35). Jesus warns that we will be forgiven in the same way that we forgive. This last sentiment is clearly articulated in what we now know as the Lord's Prayer (Matt. 6:12, 15; Luke 11:4). Jesus prays that we will be forgiven of our debts just as we forgive those who are endebted to us.

If we stop and think about it, Jesus' teaching here underscores many other important principles of the Christian faith that he taught, such as turning the other cheek, doing to others as we would like for them to do to us, and loving our neighbors as ourselves. All of these are vital elements in achieving godly partnership, but they are difficult to live out. When I write that statement I am reminded, however, that I am not alone in this venture. Not only do I have partnership with godly sisters and brothers who constantly encourage and challenge me to walk faithfully in the instruction of the Lord, but I also have the Holy Spirit living within me. As Christians we are never asked to do something that God does not equip and empower us to do. I may not have the strength, but God will supply it. I may not even have the desire, but God will form it in me.

The Holy Spirit grows fruit that is pleasing to God and to those around us: love, joy, peace, patience, kindness, generosity, faithfulness, gentleness, and self-control (Gal. 5:22–26). When other things crowd out the Spirit, however, little room remains for fruit to grow and mature. As an adult, I think I am closer to understanding what it means to have a hardened heart and how one comes into that state of being. The hardening of the heart occurs over time. It is like the formation of bedrock in a riverbed. At first only small grains of sand or fine pebbles are present—in the heart these are usually petty things, small offenses, and insignificant slights. But the more that collect and the longer they remain, they soon form a larger mass, so these once-small offenses feel like greater insults.

As larger stones collect—even deeper wounds and more profound betrayals—they bond with the growing mass to eventually form a rock solid and impenetrable barrier that fills the heart. No godly fruit can be born in this environment, and forgiveness is out of the question. We all know individuals who have hard hearts, even if we don't use this language to describe them.

Bitter, angry, critical, complaining, difficult, immovable, defensive, conflicted—the list could go on and on. Every church that I know has at least a few people with these qualities, and we rarely know how to respond to them. Partnership in these situations becomes at least undesirable, at most impossible. Many of us, unfortunately, just walk away. We are too frightened, too cowardly, or too fed up to deal forthrightly with them. If, however, we considered that perhaps their condition is because of an inability to forgive, I believe there might be hope. Of course, it would be best if we cleaned out the grains of sand and small pebbles before they formed a mass. It would also be good if we helped each other let go of the larger stones and refused to collect them in our hearts. But when we are dealing with an already hardened heart, we must look to see where forgiveness has been neither offered nor received.

If forgiveness is what we desire from God, we have clear instruction and excellent models of how we repent and confess our sins, pray for forgiveness, and receive the blessing of a restored relationship. If forgiveness is what we must offer to or receive from one another, we follow much the same path. Although certainly not easy, we at least know what to do in these situations. But what if none of them fits the hardness that remains in a person's heart? Where else might forgiveness be needed? I suggest that there are two other possibilities that must be considered.

Often I have found that deeply troubled people struggle to forgive themselves. Sometimes it is a result of perfectionism—the setting of unattainable standards that lead to constant failure. At other times, it is because of a particular sin—one that they believe is inexcusable and unforgiveable. Still others are unable to forgive themselves because someone significant in their lives also refuses to forgive them—in these cases, the offender joins rank with the offended in believing that forgiveness is not possible. In so doing, they validate the refusal to forgive, and the vicious cycle continues. Walking gently but firmly with these individuals and guiding them to self-forgiveness is both a challenging and rewarding ministry. The community of faith must realize the great need for such ministries of deliverance and offer hope and help to those unable to forgive themselves or others.

The other place that we rarely consider granting forgiveness is to God. I have known far too many dear people who have no idea that they live in this state. They walk around with heavy hearts and little joy, often beating themselves up because they struggle with doubt and fear. They use their anger and frustration to fuel their dissatisfaction with God and everything associated with religion. Or they walk away completely and never look back; faith offers no meaning and God no hope. Many of these people have bargained with God and lost. God has disappointed them, hurt them, refused to protect them, failed in responding to their prayers, taken someone or something away from them, left too many questions unanswered, the list goes on. So what do we do in these situations? I think we follow the same course we would in restoring any relationship.

Sometimes just acknowledging that we are deeply angry with or disappointed in God is itself a form of healing. At other times, the healing process takes much longer. We may have to prayerfully and faithfully wait until the struggling person is ready to forgive God. Whatever we do, I think it is most important that we not give up on these brothers and sisters. Although they may be difficult to partner with, they certainly are in need of committed relationships that will stand with them no matter what the outcome. This kind of dedication is only possible when we decide that forgiveness, grace, mercy, love—all of the attributes of Jesus—really are our way of life, and that we want to embrace them fully to become more like him.

Thoughts on Working Together

"Because of the two guys and one girl that were in my group I looked forward to our service time. Not only did we work together, but we also edified and encouraged one another. There were times when we were very serious and dug deep into certain areas that we were going through or would someday go through. There were also times we would almost fall out of our chairs because we were laughing so hard. . . . [Through this project,] I had the privilege of working with what I now would consider three very close friends."

—Male Student

Forgiveness as a Way of Life

The apostle Paul wrote from prison to the church at Philippi, his partner in the gospel, encouraging them to stand firmly together no matter what the circumstances (1:27–30). Familiar with relational difficulties of all kinds, Paul encouraged the Philippians to follow the sacrificial, humble example of Jesus and to look to others who lived similar lives (2:1–11, 19–30). After sharing his own desire to better know Christ at any cost, he gets down to the specific situation that is troubling the church: two of his co-workers, Euodia and Syntyche, were in discord and it affected the whole church (4:1–3).

In the middle of a study of Philippians, I discovered something significant about partnership that has really blessed my life. I was home for the afternoon and picked up a magazine with a leading article entitled "Laws of Lasting Love."[1] I generally dismiss such reading because it seems too shallow and simplistic, but I just wanted to relax for a few minutes, so I sat down to read. The second law really caught my attention: "In crisis, become as one." The author shared a couple of stories about couples that learned how to really be united through crises in their lives. All of a sudden, I made two significant connections—one about the epistle and one about a personal relationship.

Paul wanted the Philippians to understand that unity in the body of Christ is most needed when conflict arises, and it is possible for us to pull together because of our relationship with the Lord. In these instances, we are called to lay aside everything trivial, to forgive any leftover hurts, and to focus on what is of greatest importance. Yet I rarely united with Jack when we were in disagreement with each other. Rather, I would pull away in self-protection or lash out angrily to keep him at bay. As a child growing up in an alcoholic home, I learned to take care of myself, a good survival technique early on but a destructive reaction for a mature adult. Reflecting on this article in relationship to the epistle helped me see that walking in the way of Jesus means we always have a choice in how we respond in any situation. The Lord can reform even our innate responses and bad habits. Even though I now apply this message to my interpersonal relationships, it is equally significant for our churches.

Good and godly choices are what Paul encouraged Euodia and Synthyce, and the whole congregation at Philippi, to make. He wanted readers to find joy in the Lord, something he had done even while in prison (see 4:4; also 1:18b and 2:17b). He challenged readers to be gentle because the Lord is near—Jesus is close by and he is coming again. Paul instructed readers not to worry about anything but to express concerns in thankful prayer (4:5–6). Finally, Paul exhorted readers to think only of what was true, honorable, just, pure, pleasing, commendable, excellent, and worthy of praise. All of these choices are integral to living out the character of Christ and to honoring him with our lives and relationships. The promises connected to making these qualities our way of life are that the "peace of God" will guard our hearts and minds in Christ Jesus (4:7) and the "God of peace" will be with us (4:9). This order is a tall one. I have already confessed my struggles in living up to these standards, and yet I believe it is possible in light of the forgiveness I have received and in the forgiveness I offer to others.

Filtering these lessons into my daily life, however, can be a real challenge. One time, my friend Amber and I, along with several others, were leading a women's Bible study at a missions conference in Thailand. Just before she was to teach, Amber, who is several years younger than I am, asked how I decided how much of myself to share in these kinds of situations. I told her that through the years, I learned to trust the Spirit to lead me in being just who I am, and that I live always prepared to apologize when I cause offense to others. For some reason, these words really resonated with Amber, and she told me later that she reflected on them for weeks. She reported that living with this perspective was very liberating for her. In further discussion, we shared how this way of thinking and acting empowered us to make forgiveness more of a constant in our lives. If *we live always ready to ask for and receive forgiveness*, our partnerships can be stronger and even deeper. We also grow in greater awareness of how we affect our partners and can, therefore, be even more sensitive toward them.

Much of what I shared with Amber initially was what I had learned through trial and error. Early in my life, I grew predominantly through personal experience. As I matured in Christ, however, I began to understand that I needed to be more intentional about spiritual growth. I would like to close this chapter with some specific practices that have helped me grow spiritually in my relationships with God and with others.

To begin with, *we can choose a specific characteristic of God to be the focus of our spiritual discipline*. So, for example, when I want to become more forgiving, I purposefully focus my attention in that direction. In my prayer life, I joyfully praise God's forgiving nature, I deeply thank God for the many ways that I have experienced divine forgiveness, and I humbly confess the areas in which I still need God's forgiveness. In my study, I look at texts that speak of God's forgiveness—especially narratives, psalms, and parables. As I reflect and journal on what God is teaching me about forgiveness, my heart becomes tender toward others, even those whom I might consider enemies. I even seem better equipped to forgive myself. With this intentionality, forgiveness begins flowing in every dimension of my life.

It was in such a time of deliberate discipline that I once again realized how burdened I had let myself become, unable to let go and trust God. In many ways, I resembled women that many of us have seen in third world countries, bent over and unable to stand because they carry such unbelievably heavy loads. Although physically fine, spiritually I was a bent-over woman. Each morning and evening, I would come to the Lord in prayer, unburdening my heart and life. I would carefully lay down everything that concerned me and everyone that I loved. I would stretch my spiritual muscles, feeling momentary relief as I talked with the Lord. Then I would prepare to leave, placing it all back on myself, a perfect fit. After all, these were my concerns, my relationships.

Then one morning, God instructed me to leave it all. I could not imagine what that meant and felt empty and confused as I prepared to go to work. Throughout the day, I found myself "picking up" various burdens and carrying them around with me. Yet each time, the message from the Lord was the same, "Let go and trust me to take care of everything that is important to you; they are even more important to me." For the next several weeks, I continued to struggle with surrender. But what I learned during that period of time was the joy of having a light step and a free heart in the Lord. It was like coming out of a long illness and finally feeling healthy again. It is true that *we must learn to surrender every burden to God* if we intend to walk in the way of the Lord more fully.

As I grew in this practice of trusting and leaving everything with God, I discovered deeper burdens from the past that I did not realize I was still carrying. The most difficult place to surrender for me was in past relationships. I felt the need to confront various individuals about some past hurts or injuries if I was going to reestablish meaningful partnership. Having such a meeting, a "carefrontation,"[2] can be a healing and blessing for all concerned. Yet such a conversation is not always possible because the person is unavailable or unwilling. These realities caused me to look for other ways to address the situations. First, of course, I can ask for direction or help from fellow believers. Second, I become a *coach to myself*. After praying about a situation and still needing to figure out what direction to take, I often practice self-talk. The question I most frequently ask myself is, "As Jeanene's best friend, what do you think she especially needs to hear from you on this subject?" My responses vary, but they always have to do with my attitude, my choices, and my perspective—all realms in which I can address any difficult situation by dealing with my stuff.

Third, I have tried an *empty chair approach*. A beloved counselor and friend taught this technique to me. He suggested that I use my imagination to place the person I needed to talk with in an empty chair. (I found it most useful to have a trusted friend or therapist with me to listen in and give guidance.) There, I shared all of my feelings and frustrations. Although I do not truly know how the other would respond to the situation, I at least experienced release of any negative emotions that were harbored in my spirit. The whole experience has proven to be a source of healing for me, and I hope it will also bless others.

Even after I finished therapy, I still struggled to understand the limitations of others in expressing love, forgiveness, and acceptance. One day, I prayed that I be allowed to see two specific individuals *with God's eyes*. I based my request on Paul's writing to the church at Corinth:

From now on, therefore, we regard no one from a human point of view; even though we once knew Christ from a human point of view, we know him no longer that way. So if anyone is in Christ, there is a new creation: everything old has passed away; see everything has been made new! (2 Cor. 5:16–17)

Thoughts on Working Together

"[I] learned through this project [that accountability] is a vital part of effective partnership. A partnership is made or broken by the commitment level of each member. True partnership in ministry cannot take place if half the partnership is not present, doing their share, having a positive attitude, etc. It is the responsibility of partners to hold each other accountable to the commitments the team has made. We must be willing to accept criticism and motivation from each other. We must be ready to stand up and confront in love a team member who isn't fulfilling his or her obligations. I feel that we did not do this as effectively as we could have.... In the future I personally want to work on my fear of confrontation, and learn to come to friends and co-workers with the proper attitude and motivate them to 'stay the course.'"

—Female Student

And God granted my request. For just a moment, I saw the two wounded, neglected, abused, and unloved children that these people had been. Simultaneously, I was allowed to see the transformed people whom God was making them into. My heart was full of compassion, empathy, and great love for both of them, and I was freed of expecting from them what they have been unable or unwilling to give to our relationship. I know that

God was, and is still, in the process of working in their lives and mine. I also know that God can be trusted completely to bring the transformation of all our lives "to completion by the day of Christ Jesus" (Phil. 1:6).

When Paul challenged the quarreling Euodia and Syntyche to "be of the same mind in the Lord," he also asked the whole church—his loyal companion—to assist them in doing so (Phil. 4:2–3). Godly, effective partnership is best achieved in the community of faith. There, acceptance is given to each person in the partnership based on the value we are given in Christ Jesus. There, appreciation for gifts and contributions is extended because the whole body benefits from them. And there, accountability is offered to help each of us grow in areas of strength and overcome in areas of weakness.

Conclusion

The morning that I learned, rather than taught, about forgiveness was just the introduction of how vital it is in my life. As I have indicated throughout this chapter, I am a person with many flaws and in need of much forgiveness. I thank God daily that I do not have to do it all on my own. I have not only the power of God to bless me, but also the company of many wonderful brothers and sisters in Christ. I continue to grow in my Christian walk and in the significant partnerships of my life.

Writing this book has been a ten-year journey for me. It began as the basis of the project thesis for my Doctor of Ministry degree. It became a significant portion of equipping men and women in the undergraduate department in which I taught. It grew into a longitudinal study about how partnership is formed between men and women. As it ends, I find myself feeling both grieved and relieved.

These past several years, I have longed to be released from a directive from God to do this work. At times, I simply had to put it down and walk away—it was too difficult to examine partnership any further. During this period, many of my partnerships have flourished but others have suffered; some have even ceased to exist. Through it all, however, I have learned to depend more deeply on God and to love others more fully—I found strength from these realities to complete the task.

Students involved in the project through the years expressed a similar range of responses to it. Several experienced immediate insight and growth through their teamwork. Others acknowledged that they learned something about partnership, but many of them did it reluctantly and some irately. I hope if they read this book, they will be blessed to know that they contributed to it significantly. Most of all, I pray that these efforts will bless men and women as they form godly partnerships in which they can learn and flourish.

Notes to Chapter Six

1. Paul Piersall, "Laws of Lasting Love," condensed in *Reader's Digest* (March 1995), 147–150.
2. A term I first learned in a course taught by Dr. Charles Siburt in my doctor of ministry program at ACU.

Original Design of the Project

The initial implementation of the project was a result of requirements for my doctoral studies. For the project thesis, I was asked to find a need within my ministry context, plan a project that would serve as an intervention, implement the project, and then evaluate its effectiveness. After reviewing the classes I teach and the overall curriculum in the Department of Bible, Missions, and Ministry, I realized that there was no concentrated effort made to train and equip majors to work together as women and men preparing for a profession in ministry or missions. The most obvious place to do this intervention was in a series of required courses that are team-taught in the spring semester of the students' junior years and the fall semester of their senior years. The majors are also required to complete a field education requirement in the form of a summer internship between the two semesters.

These courses are team-taught and are collaborative learning classrooms. Beginning in spring 2000, students in the introductory course were placed into learning teams of 3–5 diverse individuals, and they worked on various projects and assignments together that helped them develop interpersonal skills, utilize interactive strategies, and understand group dynamics. The intention of these groups was two-fold: 1) to better prepare them for the work they would do as summer interns and 2) to prepare them for better teamwork in their future work in ministry. These same learning teams carried over to the fall semester with only minor adjustments made due to enrollment variation. The model for training and experience in meaningful partnership between men and women was designed to take place in the context of these learning teams in the fall course. An integral part of this course for the previous 4–5 years has been the involvement of students in a service-learning project followed by a reflection paper on their experience. This assignment seemed to be the natural place to do more training for and gain experience in working toward greater partnership for men and women because a teamwork component was already in place, but the teaching team agreed that it needed a major revision. Other good reasons to continue the service-learning project were new initiatives under way at that time at Abilene Christian University and many other institutions of higher learning to make service-learning an integral part of a student's educational experience and the core curriculum.[1]

The first activity the learning teams were asked to complete on an individual basis was a pre-project questionnaire that allowed students in the learning teams to begin thinking about how they would define meaningful partnership and evaluate the interaction of their specific learning team accordingly. Their reflection then became the starting point of their group discussion about these important matters in an interactive class section. The pre-project questionnaire also provided a point of comparison for how they felt prior to the class presentations and a post-project questionnaire helped them determine how they grew through this process. Both the pre- and post-project questionnaires were intended to assist students in writing insightful reflection papers on the whole group project and to determine how well they achieved meaningful partnership with one another. Two ninety-minute interactive sessions were conducted during the scheduled class time, drawing on relevant reading assignments. The first interactive session began with each learning team sharing their pre-questionnaire responses with their group; we the professors then gave an overview of theological perspectives on partnership. The class concluded with the learning teams evaluating their strengths and weaknesses, setting goals for their work together, and spending time in prayer.

The second interactive session focused first on students' responses to their assigned reading. Next, the class discussed the basic assumptions of this project about men and women and the principles they thought should be integral for forming godly partnership between men and women. Finally, each learning team received three handouts: 1) a list of opportunities from *ACU's Volunteer Center,* developed especially for this course; 2) a *Project Completion Report,* to be used for turning in the hours spent in the project and verification by an on-site supervisor; and 3) an *Informed Consent Document,* to be completed before students signed up to participate in focus groups to evaluate and discuss the project.

The second phase of the project required each learning team to work in partnership to plan, execute, and evaluate their service-learning project. Each learning team had to meet outside of class to determine how they would begin their service-learning project and when they would initiate contact with their community service agency. Several possible ideas for the service project at each site had been discussed with Nancy Coburn, director of the Volunteer Service-Learning Center at ACU, and the contact person for each agency. The intention of offering several possibilities for each project allowed the learning teams to select an option that best suited them, provided opportunities for each agency to express their specific needs in the process, and opened the door for the learning teams and agencies to forge unique partnerships.

Phase three of the project was the evaluation of students' service-learning projects, reflection on their work together as learning teams, and assessment of how well they achieved meaningful partnership in the process.

The primary means for evaluation of the training and experience of partnership within the service-learning project was through focus groups. Since the design of the project was conducted in learning teams, this form of qualitative research provided a unique opportunity to examine students' experiences and perspectives in a way that would not be possible without group interaction.[2] In their work on the value of focus groups, David L. Morgan and Richard A. Krueger suggest that understanding the complex behavior of participants may require more than one means of examining that behavior and recommend that focus groups may need to be combined with other forms of qualitative research. Yet in a later publication, Morgan acknowledges that "... focus groups, like other qualitative methods, can be a well-chosen, self-contained means for collecting research data."[3] Thomas W. Lee notes in his book that the interactive nature of the discussion "... that takes place in focus groups—in which members share and compare their experiences, resulting in potentially powerful social facilitation—can provide researchers with substantial insight into group-level phenomena."[4]

For this project, the focus group discussion was designed so that it began broadly, asking for initial impressions, followed by unexpected realizations. The discussion then narrowed to the identification of elements that participants thought were critical for good partnership between men and women, followed by a rating of their own learning team's development of such a partnership. The final component was advice that participants would give to others seeking to form such partnerships in the future.

Three quality checks were also put into place, however, to ensure the validity of data gathered from the focus groups. One check was the addition of an extra focus group, comprised of representatives from the community service providers who observed the learning teams as they conducted the service-learning projects with their agencies. These professionals possess a degree of objectivity not possible among project participants. Comparison of the insights from this focus group with those conducted with student participants helped ensure reliable data. Also, the requirement of 5–7 page individual reflection papers one week after the final focus group allowed students to express opinions and concerns that might not have been possible within the dynamic of the focus groups.[5] Finally, member checks of the initial research data from the focus groups were conducted with select members of each learning team to ensure "that the representation constructed by the [researcher was] credible to participants."[6]

Notes to the Appendix

1. The mission of ACU is to educate students for Christian service and leadership throughout the world. The broad mission of the Department of Undergraduate Bible is to provide biblical training, Christian spiritual formation, and a Christian worldview for every student in the university.

2. We also decided to use focus groups because, as David L. Morgan and Richard A. Krueger write in "When to Use Focus Groups and Why," "[b]y comparing the different points of view that participants exchange during their interactions in focus groups, [the researcher] can examine motivation with a degree of complexity that is typically not available with other methods." In addition, when the researcher's ". . . goal is to modify behavior that depends on complex information flow or a mix of attitudes, knowledge, and past experiences, then focus groups can provide [her] with a tool that is uniquely suited to the task." Finally, focus groups can be conducted in a timely, efficient, and low-cost manner that is particularly conducive to the learning environment of the university. See David L. Morgan and Richard A. Krueger, "When to Use Focus Groups and Why," in *Successful Focus Groups: Advancing the State of the Art*, ed. David L. Morgan (Newbury Park: Sage, 1993), 16.

3. David L. Morgan, *Focus Groups as Qualitative Research*, 2nd ed., Qualitative Research Methods Series, vol. 16 (Thousand Oaks: Sage, 1997), 18.

4. Thomas W. Lee, *Using Qualitative Methods in Organizational Research*, Organizational Research Methods Series (Thousand Oaks: Sage, 1999), 52.

5. We felt that this additional assignment was particularly necessary to ensure a voice for the female participants in this project. The male-female ratio in most classes was 6-1, most of the students were unmarried, and the university they were attending is biblically conservative—all factors we felt might inhibit full expression of these women's opinions, and so we wanted to provide an additional outlet to promote freedom of expression.

6. Mary Jane Brotherson and Beth L. Goldstein, "Quality Design of Focus Groups in Early Childhood Special Education Research," *Journal of Early Intervention*, 16.4 (1992): 338.

Study Guide

CHAPTER ONE

For Small Group Discussion:

1. Describe a "sacred moment" that you have experienced in partnership with Christian women or men. What made the experience possible? Why was it significant for you?

2. How do you respond to the author's assertion that the creation accounts in Genesis 1 and 2 are intended more to teach us about who God is than to document what happened each day? What difference does such an approach make in understanding these passages? in how we teach them?

3. What do you think it means for men and women to be made in God's image? Examine endnote 4, in which Rick Marrs presents an alternate understanding of some elements of the creation story. How do you respond to these interpretations?

4. What difference does it make to realize that, unlike the earth and the serpent, humanity was not cursed? that the pronouncements of Genesis 3 are descriptive rather than prescriptive?

5. How do you respond to the assertion that the effects of sin are limited (only to the third or fourth generation) but that the blessings of faithfulness are endless (to the thousandth

generation)? What difference does this understanding make in how we view the past? the present? the future? How does this perspective inform our partnerships?

6. What do you find noteworthy in the discussion in Chapter One about partnerships in the Hebrew Bible? in the new order of the New Testament?

7. Close by sharing what insights or connections you gathered from this chapter and how they affect your partnerships now and in the future.

For Personal Reflection:

1. Reflect on the partnerships in which you participate— at home, at work, and in the community of faith—and how what you have read in this chapter might affect each relationship.

2. Pray about your partnerships, your place in them, and how you would like them grow in greater godliness.

CHAPTER TWO

For Small Group Discussion:

1. Examine the definition of partnership in this chapter. On a scale of 1 to 5 (where 1 is strongly agree and 5 is strongly disagree), how would you rate your response to it? Why?

2. Consider the author's call for Christian women to repent and reclaim a loving stance toward others in each of the following areas. What connections do you make with each one?

   a. Practice of misandry—

   b. Tendency toward misogyny—

   c. Misunderstanding of headship/submission—

   d. Propensity toward unhealthy helpfulness—

   e. Unwillingness to address weakness/sin with Christian brothers—

   f. Prevalence of inappropriate romantic expectations—

g. Inability to deal with negative emotions—

h. Failure to acknowledge God-given gifts and talents and use them for God's glory—

3. In what other areas do you see the need for Christian women to repent and reclaim so they can better participate in godly partnerships?

4. Turn your attention to the author's call for Christian men to repent and reclaim a loving stance toward others. What connections do you make with each of the following?

a. Practice of self-degradation—

b. Tendency to adopt gender specific qualities/stereotypes—

c. Participation in misogyny/misandry—

d. Misunderstanding of headship/submission—

e. Failure to take responsibility for providing appropriate comfort, shelter, or protection—

    f. Acceptance of secular views of male ego and male libido—

    g. Hesitancy to confront Christian sisters with their weaknesses and sin—

    h. Propensity of some men to dominate and control—

5. In what other areas do you see the need for Christian men to repent and reclaim so they can better participate in godly partnerships?

6. Close the group discussion with prayer for each member and their functions in godly partnership.

For Personal Reflection:

1. Begin with a centering prayer that focuses on the unity and harmony that can only be found in Christ.

2. Continue the prayer by focusing on the areas in which you need to repent and reclaim what God wants in your relationships. (Christian women should look at the areas of repentance listed in question 2 of the group discussion questions,

Christian men should look at those listed in question 4.) Pray for God's grace and forgiveness.

3. Determine if there is any other course of action needed and how you will carry it out.

CHAPTER THREE

For Small Group Discussion:

1. Share a time when telling your story or hearing the story of another changed the way you related to one another.

    a. What are the obstacles that keep us from telling our stories to each other? What can we do to overcome them?

    b. What happens to our understanding of ourselves when we see our stories as a continuation of God's story? What effect does it have on our relationships with each other?

2. What difference would it make in our relationships if we saw growing closer to Christ and each other as a central purpose of relationships? How would it affect the ways in which we accomplish our tasks?

3. Why do you think communication is a challenging part of most of our relationships? What do you think of the author's suggestions about the following?

    a. Considering the diverse make-up of a group—

    b. Praying for and with one another—

    c. Forming a spiritual covenant—

    d. Being open with one another—

    e. Listening intently to each other—

4. What experiences do you have with groups that modeled the following types of leadership? What would it look like for someone to step up or step down in each instance?

    a. Default method—

    b. Democratic approach—

    c. No-leadership model—

    d. Maternal leadership model—

    e. Collaborative approach—

5. Describe situations in which you have experienced the under- or over-functioning of others. What about those in which you have under- or over-functioned? How can learning to

be responsible for self alter these tendencies? What can Christian brothers and sisters do to help one another in these areas?

6. Why are we frequently tempted to present ourselves as "having it all together" instead of as people who really struggle? What difference does grace make in our lives? in our partnerships?

For Personal Reflection:

1. Reflect on which elements of godly partnership are more challenging to you and why.

   a. Sharing your story

   b. Finding the center

   c. Learning to communicate

   d. Knowing when to step up or step down

   e. Giving grace to all

2. Pray about your response and share it with a close friend this week. Ask him/her to hold you accountable as you strive to grow in this area of your life.

CHAPTER FOUR

For Small Group Discussion:

1. Why do you think Christians often struggle with culture and their responses to it?

2. As you review the possible responses to culture listed below, which one would you say best represents you? Why do you think that is true? Which one do you think best describes how your church primarily interacts with culture? Why?

    a. Rejecting the culture:

        - Complete separation

        - Ignoring culture

    b. Altering culture:

        - Change the culture

        - Manipulate the culture

    c. Appreciating culture:

        - Debate the culture

        - Baptize the culture

3. How is your view of culture affected by the assumption that God designed and rules over all cultures? What differences do these ideas make in your ability to critically engage culture?

4. How do you respond to the notion that gender is a social or cultural construct? to the ideas that neither the social sciences nor Scripture can be used to give clear and distinguishable roles for either gender?

5. As you consider churches that lead the way, what strengths do you see in your own congregation? What unique challenges do you face?

    a. Churches that understand that timing is everything—

    b. Churches that wait for the leading of the Spirit—

    c. Churches that understand the importance of prayer—

    d. Churches that value unity in diversity—

    e. Churches that handle conflict well—

6. Based on your responses to question 5, where would you like to see greater growth for your community of faith? Why do you think growth in this area is important? What impact would it have on the surrounding culture? on the development of effective partnerships between women and men?

For Personal Reflection:

1. Reflect on what you have learned about your view of culture and willingness to critically engage it. What are the obstacles you face? Where are there opportunities?

2. Pray about your discoveries and the differences they can make in your life and relationships.

CHAPTER FIVE

For Small Group Discussion:

1. The author asserts that even though Christians do not embrace the secular views of marriage presented in this chapter, they are still influenced by them. Do you agree or disagree? Explain your answer.

2. How do you react to the suggestion that "the family that prays together, stays together" is a pseudo-Christian view of marriage? That it can even be a form of idolatry?

3. What is your response to the idea that spouses who focus too much time and energy on Christian service are committing spiritual adultery? How might the church partner with marriages in which this problem occurs?

4. On a scale of 1 to 5 (where 1 is strongly agree and 5 is strongly disagree), do you agree with the sense that the "one-flesh" perspective of marriage best fits God's design for it?

    a. What are your points of greatest agreement? What are the strengths of this view?

    b. Where do you find yourself disagreeing with this perspective? What do you find troubling in it?

5. In Chapter Two, the author called both Christian men and women to repent of views of headship/submission that harm their relationships with one another. In this chapter, she presents an alternative view that she considers biblical.

    a. What are your points of greatest agreement? What are the strengths of this view?

    b. Where do you find yourself disagreeing with this perspective? What do you find troubling in it?

6. In the final section of this chapter, three principles are given indicating how God uses marriage to teach us to be holy. Share experiences in which you have seen marriage teach people:

    a. To love like God loves—

    b. To be faithful as God is faithful—

    c. To bear witness to God's activity in our lives—

7. In what other ways do you see God using marriage to make us more holy?

For Personal Reflection:

1. Reflect on how your understanding of Christian marriage has been challenged or enriched by this chapter. In what areas do you need to give special attention to your own marriage or to serve others in theirs?

2. Spend time in prayer about what you have learned, what you need to put into practice, and whom you need to share these things with.

CHAPTER SIX

For Small Group Discussion:

1. What difference would it make if we all had a sign around our necks stating "Work in Progress"? Why is it often easy for us to forget this reality in our interpersonal relationships?

2. Which of the two realities of forgiveness given in this chapter is most difficult for you?

   a. That forgiveness is a great gift we are given that must be received—

   b. That forgiveness is a great gift that we in turn give to others—

3. How do you respond to the idea that forgiveness, like our salvation and healing, is an ongoing event? How does it help or hinder you in receiving and giving forgiveness?

4. Why is it difficult for us to forgive people who do not ask for our forgiveness? What do you think of the author's assertion that we must offer forgiveness whether the other repents or not?

5. Why is it often difficult to forgive ourselves? Do you agree with the author's statement that failure to do so is suggesting to God that this sin needs more than all of the blood of Christ to be forgiven? How does this thinking potentially affect our partnerships?

6. On a scale of 1 to 5 (where 1 is strongly agree and 5 is strongly disagree), how would you rate your response to each of the following ideas?

   a. That our inability to forgive one another is one of the greatest barriers to our partnerships—

   b. That sometimes it is God who needs our forgiveness—

   c. That often what lies behind difficult people is an inability or unwillingness to give or receive forgiveness—

7. Consider which of the spiritual disciplines mentioned at the end of the chapter might be useful for you to put into practice and why:

   a. Choosing a specific characteristic of God to be the focus of your devotional life—

b. Surrendering every burden to God and leaving it with God—

c. Having a "carefrontation" with a person with whom you struggle—

d. Asking other Christians for direction or help—

e. Serving as a coach to yourself through self-talk—

f. Using the empty chair approach—

g. Praying to see those who have offended you through God's eyes—

For Personal Reflection:

1. Reflect on how you would respond to the question found in the opening story of this chapter: "Have you ever had a situation in which you found it especially difficult to forgive?" Spend time in prayer about your response.

2. Review question 7 under the group discussion section and choose one of the spiritual disciplines for your personal use in a particularly troubled situation.